Critical Guides to German Texts

13 Lenz: Der Hofmeister

Critical Guides to German Texts

EDITED BY MARTIN SWALES

LENZ

Der Hofmeister

Edward McInnes

Professor of German
University of Hull

Grant & Cutler Ltd
1992

© Grant & Cutler Ltd 1992

ISBN 0 7293 0342 X

I.S.B.N. 84-599-3261-3
DEPÓSITO LEGAL: V. 518 - 1992

Printed in Spain by
Artes Gráficas Soler, S.A., Valencia
for
GRANT & CUTLER LTD
55-57 GREAT MARLBOROUGH STREET, LONDON, W1V 2AY

For Fiona and Matthew

9th August 1991

Contents

Acknowledgements

I would like to express my thanks to Mrs Catherine Ready for taking on the preparation of the manuscript despite the pressure of all her other duties, and for completing the task with her usual relaxed and calming efficiency. I also feel indebted to Professor Martin Swales for his generous interest and editorial advice. I am also pleased to acknowledge the stimulus I received from the students in my final-year 'Age of Goethe' seminar, who clearly didn't believe everything I told them.

E. McI.

Prefatory Note

The page numbers in brackets refer to J.M.R. Lenz, *Der Hofmeister oder Vorteile der Privaterziehung* (Stuttgart: Reclam, 1963). Other references, indicated in brackets by italicized figures, are to the numbered items in the Select Bibliography.

Introduction

Der Hofmeister is often described in histories of literature as 'a drama of the *Sturm und Drang*'. No doubt this description serves some rough-and-ready function within literary periodization, but it seems to me to do scant justice to Lenz's play and to be in fact quite misleading in some respects. It appears to imply that *Der Hofmeister* was a work which arose out of the momentum of a concerted literary movement and contributed in some recognizable way to its corporate aims and endeavours. Such an impression would be quite false. In the first place (as we shall see later) Lenz wrote this his first play almost completely within a year of coming to Straßburg in the summer of 1771. During this year, burdened as he was by his obligations as a 'lackey-companion' to the von Kleist brothers, he came into contact only gradually with the other young writers like Goethe, Jung-Stilling, Klinger and Wagner, as well as more established figures like Herder and Salzmann - the group which later came to be known as the *Stürmer und Dränger* (*10*, pp.89ff.; *27*, pp.16f.). All the evidence suggests that Lenz's early relations with the members of this group were tentative and probing, and that neither he nor any of the others had the sense of participating in a progressing, collaborative venture.

We must also bear in mind that at the time when Lenz was writing *Der Hofmeister* no member of this group had as yet actually published a play. Goethe, it is true, had begun work on *Götz von Berlichingen* in this period and may even (although there is no record of this) have discussed his plans with Lenz, but his drama did not appear in print till 1773 (*10*, p.86). It was also only in this year, as Trunz reminds us, that there is the first recorded mention of Goethe's Faust drama (*3*, Vol.3, p.421). All the best known and most representative plays of the *Sturm und Drang* (with the obvious

exception of *Götz* and the *Urfaust*) were written towards the middle
of the decade: plays like Leisewitz's *Julius von Tarent*, Klinger's *Die
Zwillinge* and *Sturm und Drang*, Wagner's *Die Kindermörderin* and
Lenz's *Die Soldaten*, all of which were published in 1776.

It is important to remember these facts in order to appreciate
the extent to which *Der Hofmeister* was a pioneering, initiating
work. It sounded new formal possibilities and modes of social
presentation which were ahead of their time, so much so indeed that
they were to influence developments in the drama less in the 1770s
than in the next century.

The tendency to see *Der Hofmeister* as an exemplary work of
the *Sturm und Drang* is misleading in one other very important
respect. The impetus of this movement (as I have tried to show in
detail elsewhere) sprang from the fundamental, intuitive
commitment of all its participants to the creative potentialities of the
individual (*35*, pp.15ff.). What drew these questing young writers
together was not the awareness of shared ideological concerns, much
less a desire to pool their energies in common literary or social
endeavours but, paradoxically, the relentless inward drive to artistic
self-realization which each felt in himself and acknowledged in the
others. This is reflected in the strangely loose, if often intense, nature
of their association. It is instructive, I think, to compare the *Sturm
und Drang* with literary movements in the 19th century like *Das
junge Deutschland* or Naturalism with which it seems at first sight to
have close affinities. The emergence of the *Sturm und Drang* seems
in contrast to these later movements quite spontaneous, unregulated
and conspicuously lacking in effective organizational focus or
direction. The young writers in Straßburg had no inclination to form
a society or found a periodical to propagate their views, nor had they
any interest in publishing pamphlets in which they could seek to
expound a shared philosophy and to influence opinion.

This indifference or aversion to concerted collective action
reflects the strongly inner, subjective character of the aspirations
which impelled all the 'members' of the movement in one way or
another. Every one of the writers involved with the group seems in a
quite remarkable degree to have regarded his contact with the others

as a means of confronting the individuality of his own artistic will. Each sought in his encounter with the others not so much to influence and be influenced as to sharpen his sense of the uniqueness of the imaginative vision which compelled him.

This is by no means to suggest that Lenz gained little or nothing from his involvement with these like-minded, ambitious and highly gifted young writers. On the contrary, without this contact it is doubtful if he could have produced a work as idiosyncratic and uncompromising in its conception as *Der Hofmeister*. What he derived from his association with the other *Stürmer und Dränger*, however, was something very difficult to define and impossible to quantify. It seems above all to have helped sustain his belief in his own personal vision at a time of self-doubt, and to steel his nerve in the face of the widespread incomprehension and downright rejection which he feared his work would provoke.

1. Lenz, Shakespeare and the Drama

> Ach ich nahm mir vor hinabzugehn und
> ein Maler der menschlichen Gesellschaft
> zu werden: aber wer mag da malen wenn
> lauter Fratzengesichter unten anzutreffen.
>
> Lenz, *Pandamonium Germanicum*

Critics have always acknowledged that Lenz's intense involvment with Shakespeare in the early 1770s had a decisive influence on his artistic development.[1] The twenty-one-year-old who read his essay on the drama (and that largely meant Shakespeare) to the Société de Philosophie et des Belles-Lettres in the winter of 1771-1772 was, no doubt, proud of his knowledge of literary history and of his perceptiveness as a critic, but he saw himself first and foremost as an aspiring young writer who was seeking through an intensive study of the Elizabethan dramatist to discover his own role as a playwright. In trying to grasp the shaping energies of Shakespeare's creative imagination he was probing his own artistic capacities and questioning the directions his work might take. If Lenz subconsciously hoped that his investigations of Shakespearian drama would confirm his own latent impulses and predilections, he must have been sharply disconcerted. Although his encounter with the English playwright was the source of compelling imaginative inspiration, it was also to prove painful and confusing in ways which he could not have foreseen and which he found very difficult to confront. His communion with Shakespeare was the source of severe

---

[1] For a full discussion of Lenz's critical encounter with the work of Shakespeare see especially Fritz Martini (*36*, pp.159ff.) and Eva Maria Inbar (*28*, pp.15ff.). Andreas Huyssen gives a perceptive historical summary of the developing critical understanding of Lenz's dramatic theories in the past forty years or so (*27*, pp.111ff.).

self-scrutiny and of anxieties which were to beset him throughout his entire career as a dramatist.

Shakespeare for Lenz was not just the greatest playwright of the modern age but the supreme prophetic genius of Christian civilization. Only Shakespeare in his view had created the artistic means to express in timeless form the unconditioned, boundless life of the individual self. He had made the drama the organ of the consciousness of modern humanity, of man come of age, sublime in his enjoyment of his God-given freedom and his infinite, inborn creativity (*35*, pp.23ff.). Lenz saw the Elizabethan playwright above all as the creator of the heroic, autonomous individual and his awesome destiny. The dramatist's poetic power found its supreme fulfilment in the creation of characters of majestic unbroken will and limitless spiritual striving. The driving exuberance and assuredly doctrinaire tone of Lenz's reflections must have taken his listeners aback. For although both Gerstenberg in the 14th part of his *Literaturbriefe* (written in 1766) and Goethe in his *Shakespeare Rede* (1771) had celebrated the English dramatist's power to bring to life dynamic, individualized protagonists who could possess completely the mind of the reader, Lenz is saying something much more radical and provocative. He is claiming that the hero in Shakespeare's tragedy in a real sense *is* the play: that his inherent overflowing life is not just the source of the dramatic movement, its main precipitating impulse, but that this life itself constitutes the substantial action of the drama, its vital imaginative energy and its ultimate artistic *raison d'être*.

In Lenz's view Shakespeare's supreme individuals do not so much inhabit the world of the play as animate and control it. In their irresistible freedom they give life to the dramatic universe and lend it final meaning. Shakespeare's heroes express the creative genius of mankind at its highest intensity:

> Es ist die Rede von Charakteren, die sich ihre Begebenheiten erschaffen, die selbstständig und unveränderlich die ganz große Maschine selbst drehen

..., nicht von Bildern, von Marionettenpuppen - von
Menschen. (2, p.343)

The most striking aspect of these reflections is Lenz's failure to
grasp the form of Shakespearian tragedy as an organically unfolding
process of conflict. He almost completely ignores the tendency to
division and self-estrangement in the tragic protagonist to which
Lessing and other Enlightenment critics had attributed a central
importance. His individual-centred perception of Shakespeare's
drama seems in fact to preclude tragic collision in any recognizable
sense. He sees the triumphantly outreaching, creative life of the self
as the sole source of value and significance in the imaginative world
of Shakespeare, and thus inevitably reduces the forces which oppose
or qualify it to expressions of blind negation (2, pp.343, 359).

The impetus of Lenz's argument here seems to be driving him
irrevocably towards the conception of a radical tragedy of social
alienation. At the heart of his discussion is the sense of an
irreducible contradiction between the divinely ordained, intrinsic
selfhood of the hero and an impersonal, contingent world at odds
with his deepest spiritual needs. Lenz shrinks, however, from
seeking to define this sense of discrepancy, and his argument both in
his lecture and in the fuller, amended version later published remains
noticeably incomplete. His inhibitions in this respect are in striking
contrast to the breezy polemic confidence which pervades the other
parts of his discussion. We can only assume that Lenz was
disconcerted here by the nascent realization that he was broaching a
mode of tragedy which was essentially new and lacked clear
sustaining roots in the Shakespearian form. Conscious that he could
not call on the unequivocal endorsement of the English dramatist he
seems to have recoiled from pursuing his argument into a sphere of
open controversy where he was no longer sure of his ground.

These misgivings, however, probably coincided with other
powerful pressures of a quite different kind. His progressive concern
with the work of Shakespeare in the summer and autumn of 1771
overlapped with his first serious essays as a dramatist. In working on
Der Hofmeister he was forced for the first time to confront in an

immediate and practical way the nature of his own peculiar talents as a dramatist and in the process to recognize the specific, and essentially restricted, possibilities they entailed. His struggles as a practising writer evidently sharpened his awareness of the overwhelmingly realistic, satirical tendency of his creative imagination, and thus of his inescapable involvement in the prosaic narrow world of provinicial German society which he needed for his art. His ongoing struggle with the different versions of *Der Hofmeister* seems to have convinced him that the quality of his creative vision, its potential range and power were not just inadequate to the pure imaginative intensity of the tragic mode but in basic respects averse to it. His irrevocable preoccupation, as he was now forced to see, was with the socially confined and driven individual, the unremarkable man and woman who lived under the constraint of impinging forces which they could not fully recognize, much less control. These were not the 'freihandelnden, selbstständigen Geschöpfe' of Shakespearian tragedy but beings who, as he wrote shortly after the completion of *Der Hofmeister*, were bereft of inner power and spontaneity, able to function only as tiny cogs in the immense mechanical system that is the world as we know it (2, p.378).

Lenz's intense preoccupation with Shakespeare throughout this time of crucial self-discovery, served, it would seem, both to confirm this intuitive commitment to a particular kind of drama and to heighten his sense of the complex and deeply perplexing nature of this commitment. He was clearly very conscious that his imaginative sensibility drew him towards a genre which was confined in its artistic scope and moral power, and was condemned to act as a cruel parody of the highest forms of drama. Yet Lenz also recognized at the same time that the comedy for all its artistic limitations, was the only form in his age which could confront the realities of social existence in all their diverse and seemingly chaotic complexity. In this sense it was, he believed, the most contemporary and contentious dramatic mode, the mode in which the playwright in the 1770s could hope to overcome the disabling rift which had opened up between art and life, between the drama as a literary form and lived experience (*35*, pp.65f.).

In this struggle to find his role as a playwright we can see the source of Lenz's strangely ambivalent misgivings about comedy as a dramatic genre and about his own ambitions as a writer of comedy, misgivings from which he was never able to be completely free. On the one hand, he could never rid himself of an almost instinctive sense of comedy as a reductive form which engaged 'life at low tide', the essentially barren, circumstantial world of the everyday. This was a mode, he felt, which by its very existence queried the beauty and inspiring grandeur of the tragic vision, and which could grasp these only in the form of broken, distorted fragments. Comedy, as Lenz tended to see it, inevitably declared the demise of tragedy because it was no longer congruent with the outlook of contemporary man, and as such he intuitively perceived comedy as an ironic, parodistic mode driven by a fierce, yearning impotence.

On the other hand, Lenz was also aware that comedy in the late 18th century was a genre in crisis which threw down a peculiarly exhilarating challenge to the playwright. Like no dramatic mode in his time it beckoned him to breath-taking risk and experiment. The comedy was the kind of drama most responsive to social experience and, he sensed, best able to accommodate the drive to close observation and rigorous analysis characteristic of modern thought (*34*, pp.79ff.). As such it was also, as Lenz recognized, the form which called in question the basic assumptions inherited from classicist aesthetics about the character and function of the drama as the supreme literary form. All such considerations filled the young iconoclast with an intoxicating sense of challenge.

It is important to stress that, although Lenz commits himself to the comedy, he always sees the work which he will create as a quite new and radical development of the genre (*10*, pp.98f.). He recognized from the start that his would be a more realistic form which would grasp the shaping impulses of collective existence in the 1770s with a detailed, diagnostic power unknown in the German theatre; which would expose the failures of society with a critical energy which, he knows full well, will surprise and disturb spectators and readers. For despite his profound doubt and chronic self-mockery Lenz sees himself as an artist strong and original enough to throw off the constraints of all inherited traditions, to reject all models and to manipulate the accepted conventions of the theatre in a way which will demonstrate his undisputed sovereignty as a creative artist. *Der Hofmeister*, as Lenz envisages it, will be a work sui generis which will startle the literary establishment of his time and open up extensive new perspectives for the drama of the future.

2. The Genesis of Der Hofmeister

Gebt auf ein Lustspiel acht, das die
Ostermesse herauskommen wird *der
Hofmeister oder die Vortheile der
Privaterziehung*... Es wird euch ergötzen.
Goethe (letter) to Langer, 6 March 1774

Our knowledge of the writing of *Der Hofmeister* is scanty. Many
important details are unknown and will probably remain so. Some
scholars believe that Lenz had written some sketches before he left
Königsberg in the spring of 1771, while others have claimed that the
evidence for this supposition is unreliable and insist that the whole
play was written in Straßburg (*53*, pp.80f.). In the end, however,
such differences of view seem insubstantial. It is unthinkable that
Lenz left Königsberg without some fairly clear ideas about his first
serious play in his head and very likely indeed that he at least noted
some of them down in one form or another. Of much greater
importance is the fact that all critics seem agreed that the
overwhelming bulk of the first version of the play was written
between the autumn of 1771 and the summer of 1772. In October of
this year he was able to send the completed manuscript to Johann
Daniel Salzmann with the diffident hope that his highly respected
friend would find his work acceptable. This version Lenz
subsequently revised quite extensively and it was the play in this
new form which came into Goethe's hands (possibly through the
mediation of Salzmann) some time in 1773. He was clearly very
impressed by this new and quite unexpected drama and finally
managed to arrange its publication in the spring of 1774.

Throughout the writing of the play Lenz evidently strove
consistently to achieve the highest possible degree of social
immediacy. This is most strikingly apparent in his provocative

determination to use his own first hand experience in Königsberg quite openly and directly as the basis of the dramatic action. Indeed, he goes out of his way to stress the nearness of his work to what he has actually lived through, seen and heard. He presents characters and events in a way which makes it obvious to his close acquaintances that they are taken over almost unchanged from real life. His friends were nonplussed, for instance, by the directness with which he transposed his experience of university life in Königsberg into dramatic form. They saw that he was not content just to present certain student types or characteristic events of student life but had attempted to recreate actual individuals he had known (*44*, pp.196f.). On some occasions in fact he went so far as to advertise this fact by retaining the name of his real-life models. In the case of minor figures this may not have seemed very important, but Lenz had no intention of stopping here. His quest for immediate, unmistakable topicality went much further. The crucial event in the action of *Der Hofmeister*, the seduction by the tutor of the daughter of the aristocratic von Berg family, was based directly on an actual incident which was well known not just in Lenz's immediate circle but throughout the whole region and which involved a family by the name of von Berg. To make it quite clear that this decisive phase in the dramatic development re-enacted an actual event, the playwright, no doubt in the face of advice to the contrary, insisted on retaining the name von Berg. Even when he revised the play and carefully changed the names of some of the subsidiary figures in order to hide the identities of the individuals on whom they were based, Lenz steadfastly insisted on calling his protagonists von Berg and thus preserving the documentary element which gave his play that sharp provocative edge of controversy he sought.

This, however, was just one, albeit very striking, aspect of Lenz's concern for incisive social immediacy. He was attempting in *Der Hofmeister* not just to recreate his own personal experience but to explore it as a means of social investigation and critical comment. This is perhaps most evident in his conception of the figure of the tutor, Läuffer. In his portrayal of this character Lenz is out to articulate the deep feelings of shame and subjection he suffered when he filled a similar position in Königsberg. In the frustrations of the hapless Läuffer he also gives voice to his own bitter resentment at the immense difficulties faced by middle-class graduates when they tried to find secure and socially influential professional positions after leaving university (*50*, pp.146ff.). In both cases we can see that Lenz was seeking both to record his own personal experience and to observe and probe it in order to grasp wider social issues in a direct and concrete way. This is symptomatic of the powerful analytical tendency of Lenz's creative imagination. As he worked on *Der Hofmeister* he seems to have been driven increasingly to confront a consciousness of society as a monstrous, coercive force which is at work at every level of the individual's life, which possesses his deepest instincts and invades his seemingly most private emotions. Lenz certainly became more and more aware that this sense of the anonymous, moving power of society took him beyond the narrow domestic concerns of the family drama of the 1760s and drove him towards the conception of a radically empirical, deterministic mode which, he sensed, would revolutionize the contemporary understanding of the theatre in general, and comedy in particular (*35*, pp.51ff.).

In the grip of his personal experiences of injustice and conflict in everyday life Lenz was impelled increasingly, it would appear, by a quest for an embracing intellectual understanding of the position of the individual in the society of his time. The abrasive social realism to which he instinctively aspired was certainly precipitated by his anger and deep sense of disaffection, but it was also shaped by a need to analyse the socio-historical processes which controlled collective existence. Only the tense interaction of these two impulses, diverse and often in tension, he intuitively felt, could realize the challenging, idiosyncratic vision he pursued.

As his work on *Der Hofmeister* progressed Lenz seems to have experienced a growing confidence in his abilities as a playwright and in the innovative conception he attempted to realize. As he overcame considerable technical difficulties his belief in his original, challenging approach noticeably increased. Nevertheless it is clear that he was never able to free himself from the fear that his play, precisely because of its idiosyncratic novelty, would be misunderstood and misjudged. This unease is most obviously apparent in his prolonged uncertainty about how he should present his work to the public, how he should describe it in generic terms. He had deep misgivings about putting forward *Der Hofmeister* as a comedy. This, he seems to have felt, would raise expectations which were inapppropriate to his play and which might therefore deter a potential publisher and alienate the sympathy of critics, readers and of theatre-audiences. When he sent *Der Hofmeister* to Salzmann on 28th June 1772 he assumed that the recipient might be better able to respond to it if he described it as a tragedy, although he admits deep misgivings about using the term of his play (53, pp.83f.). In another letter to Salzmann some six months later he again termed his play a tragedy, although he again qualified his use of the label, this time by describing it as a 'Raritätskästchen', a term which implied that his drama was a work too idiosyncratic, too diverse, too protean to be subjected to any conventional tag. Lenz seems concerned to endorse this view on the cover-page of his final manuscript. Here in order, as it were, to keep all options open and to avoid false expectation, he defines *Der Hofmeister* as 'Lust- und Trauerspiel'. In the end, however, regaining, as it seems, the courage of his original convictions, exposing himself to misapprehension and possibly ridicule, Lenz took the plunge and called his play quite simply a comedy.

3. Analysis of the Dramatic Action

> Wo Genie ist, da ist Erfindung, da ist
> Neuheit, da ist das Original.
>> Gerstenberg, *Briefe über die*
>> *Merkenwürdigkeiten der Literatur*

Exposition (i): The Scope of the Expository Process

Exposition is in a quite novel sense the vital, impelling centre of Lenz's dramas. One of his main historical achievements as a playwright was his creation of new outreaching, open forms able to express an intricate, questioning vision of the contingency of the individual's life in the everday world of society, a vision at once sardonic and probing, driven by a will to lay bare, to dissect and unmask. Lenz's dissident, sharply ironic mode of comedy arose out of a need to sound his awareness of a fundamental disparity between the inward self with its seemingly boundless capacities of longing and desire and the determining pressures of society which embrace and shape its existence. Lenz's comic perception is fired by this sense of contradiction, by the need to explore it constantly from ironically contrasting points of view and to place it in shifting, colliding perspectives.

In *Der Hofmeister*, as in Lenz's other comedies, the exposition is long and diverse. It reaches far beyond the opening scenes of the play and develops on different levels and in various forms. This sustained, far-reaching expository concern reveals a driving imaginative will to penetrate the events enacted on stage and to probe their relation to vast, enclosing processes of causality which none of the dramatic figures can oversee, much less fully understand. Lenz — and here he does open up new analytical possibilities for the drama - conducts his exposition only to a limited extent through explicit discussion between the characters. He tends much more to uncover motive and circumstance indirectly, in ways which the dramatic figures themselves cannot recognize, over their heads, as it were, and beyond the scope of their conscious understanding.

In *Der Hofmeister* there are two main expository impulses or centres of preoccupation. Lenz is concerned throughout the play to analyse the pervading, often treacherous, hold of class-awareness and class-identity over the individual, not just in his social aims and behaviour but also in his innermost, seemingly most private feelings and aspirations. No dramatist before him had attempted to trace in such close, searching detail the manner in which the individual's involvement in the world of a particular class with its constraining weight of prejudice, assumption and expectation, enmeshed and drove him with a force he could not begin to comprehend. Here, I believe, Lenz was breaking new ground and developing important new techniques of discriminated psychological presentation.

In *Der Hofmeister* Lenz also seeks to lay bare the vulnerability of the dramatic figures from another point of view. He sees them constantly as trapped and vulnerable within the intimate, apparently reassuring realm of family existence. This does not mean that he presents the family unit as somehow separate from the momentum of the collective life of society or exempt from its powerful conditioning pressures. Lenz does, however, seem to have sensed some mysterious, inescapable force of division and conflict at work in close familial relationships which was not fully subject to analysis. He constantly apprehends the individual as supremely alone and exposed in the violent, unaccountable tensions which pervade the life of the family.

The expository process in *Der Hofmeister* embraces these two linked areas of investigation. In both cases Lenz is exploring from different angles of vision the exposure of the characters in the commonplace world of day-to-day living, and, as he later claimed, attempting to realize 'ein bedingtes Gemälde ...von Sachen, wie sie da sind' (*53*, p.107). These two preoccupations, however constantly overlap and interact. Indeed, it is true to say that they are so closely bound up, that they confirm and enforce each other with such intensity that they are often in practice barely distinguishable.

In the following discussion I have chosen to examine these two areas of the exposition separately, although I am aware that there is a certain artificiality in this procedure. This seemed to me the most clear and effective way of illuminating the disparate, questioning character of Lenz's far-reaching analytical aims in this complex and still controversial play.

Exposition (ii): Class-Awareness and Social Tension

When we open *Der Hofmeister* Lenz's reluctance to call his play a comedy seems quite perplexing. He appears in fact to have gone to some lengths to let his readers in 1774 know not just that it was a comedy but a comedy of a particularly well established and popular kind which they could recognize at once. The full title, *Der Hofmeister oder Vorteile der Privaterziehung*, suggested to his contemporaries that his play was a *Berufskomödie*, one of numerous works at this time which gave a gently ironic picture of social manners through a satirical portrayal of the outlook and behaviour of a specific profession (*14*, pp.456f.). Comedies of this type had become very well known and loved in the theatre of the 1760s, most notably Lessing's *Der junge Gelehrte* (1747), Krüger's *Die Candidaten* (1748) and *Die Geistlichen auf dem Lande* (1743) and Mylius' *Ärzte* (1745).

The fact that *Der Hofmeister* dealt with the question of education must also have helped convince Lenz's first readers that they were remaining within the realm of the familiar and the acceptable. This had been a popular subject of comedy since classical times and works like Molière's *École des Femmes* and Gottsched's *Die Hausfranzösin* (1744) were for Lenz's contemporaries acknowledged and, in their different ways, influential works. In formulating the title and sub-title of his play in such an overtly conventional way he seems to be reassuring his potential readers. This is a work, he appears to be claiming, which, like many before it, has a moral purpose but is light, gentle of touch and genial in mood. Those who open its pages (or so it might seem) can be quite certain that he will bring his characters through a series of lively complications to the happy outcome which the genre preordains.

Lenz also presents the opening scenes of the exposition in a form which seems to endorse further the impression of the essentially reassuring nature of his play. The opening scene, for instance, has the conventional character of a prologue in which, in conformity with venerable comic ritual, the hero presents himself and his circumstances to the audience in a way which enables it to understand clearly the developments which follow. As soon as Läuffer, the eponymous 'hero', begins to lay bare his feelings, however, it is clear that Lenz's seemingly timid suggestions of conformism are, in fact, a sly, ironic bluff: an attempt to catch his readers or spectators off guard and so to lay them open to the full cutting force of the character's angry, resentful view of his situation:

> Mein Vater sagt: ich sei nicht tauglich zum Adjunkt. Ich glaube, der Fehler liegt in seinem Beutel; er will keinen bezahlen. Zum Pfaffen bin ich auch zu jung, zu gut gewachsen, habe zuviel Welt gesehn, und bei der Stadtschule hat mich der Geheime Rat nicht annehmen wollen. Mag's! Er ist ein Pedant, und dem ist freilich der Teufel selber nicht gelehrt genug. Im halben Jahr hätt' ich doch wieder eingeholt, was ich von der Schule mitgebracht, und dann wär' ich für einen Klassenpräzeptor noch immer viel zu gelehrt gewesen...
> (p.5)

There is certainly nothing roguish or engaging about these reflections of Läuffer's. He appears rather as a man seized by outrage, who feels himself blocked and stifled by those who exercise power over his life. He clearly regards his life as a tutor as a kind of imprisonment in which all his finest powers fester, yet from which there seems no escape (p.9). His father, the Pastor, Läuffer bitterly reflects, has thwarted his longing for an academic career on the grounds that he lacks the necessary intellectual ability. He is convinced that his father's scepticism masks a foregone refusal of a miserly old man to give his son the financial support he needs to achieve a respected and fulfilling position at university.

Meanwhile the Geheimrat von Berg, the brother of Läuffer's employer, the Major, has refused even to consider him as a candidate for the vacant teaching position at the local school, even though there seems to be no other suitable applicant. This twofold rejection has had a deeply depressing effect on the tutor and made him all the more aware of the Major's reluctance to use his influence to help Läuffer find a permanent position in the civil service, as he had secretly hoped.

The sheer injustice of all this threatens to overwhelm Läuffer. These three men, each in his position of secure social authority, have in some way, he feels, conspired to do him down, to condemn him to languish in his futile disabling existence. It is only the force of his bitter vindictive anger, it seems, which keeps him going. His reflections are brought to an end by a small, inconsequential yet supremely telling incident. Läuffer sees the two von Berg brothers coming down the street. As they approach him his words of hatred are transformed as if by some involuntary reflex into gestures of extravagant servility. The two aristocrats, however, affect not to see him and pass by without acknowledging his presence (pp.5, 6).

In this tiny, seemingly negligible event Lenz contrives to expose the full depths of Läuffer's predicament. The unthinking ease with which he falls into postures of craven self-abasement reveals a despairing impotence which is eroding the integrity of his selfhood. At the same time this encounter (or rather non-encounter) shows up the contemptuously indifferent detachment of those who have control over Läuffer's life to what is happening quite literally before their eyes: it reveals an inability or refusal on the part of the two upper-class brothers to recognize the anguish of a man who is their social inferior.

The next two scenes of exposition (I,1 and I,2) serve in different ways to explore the position of the private tutor from the point of view of the aristocratic family he serves. In both Lenz

conspicuously follows procedures of discussion inherited from
Englightenment comedy in order once again to enforce the more
sharply his own deeply critical perception of society. In the former
scene (quite surprisingly in view of what we have just witnessed) he
casts the Geheimer Rat in the traditional role of the *raisonneur*, the
clear-sighted, fair-minded individual who exposes with choric
authority the unreason and confusion in the attitudes of other
dramatic figures. He it is who challenges the Major to give clear
pedagogic and social reasons for his engagement of a private tutor:

> Du mußt doch eine Absicht haben, wenn du einen
> Hofmeister nimmst und den Beutel mit einemmal so
> weit auftust, daß dreihundert Dukaten herausfallen. Sag
> mir, was meinst du mit dem Geld auszurichten; was
> foderst du dafür von deinem Hofmeister? (p.6)

The main expository purpose of this scene (as of the one which
follows) is to show that the desire of the Major and his wife to have
a private tutor does not stem from an interest in the education of
their children. From the conversation between the two brothers it
becomes more and more obvious that the Major has never even
considered Läuffer's activities as the teacher of his offspring. When
the Geheimer Rat asks him the most fundamental of questions: 'Aber
was soll er deinen Sohn lehren?', the Major is completely taken
aback by what he sees as the extremely bizarre nature of the question
(p.5). His brother persists in his inquisition, however, and puts his
query in another way. What, he asks the Major, does he expect in
return for the salary he pays his tutor? At this his brother takes flight
into evasive and quite meaningless generalities:

> Daß er - was ich - daß er meinen Sohn in allen
> Wissenschaften und Artigkeiten und Weltmanieren - Ich
> weiß auch nicht, was du immer mit deinen Fragen willst;
> (p.6)

The Geheimer Rat sees his brother's blustering discomfiture here as confirming his view that he, the Major, has engaged a tutor because this is the accepted practice in upper-class households and represents a sign of patrician distinction. The Geheimer Rat is making clear to the reader or spectator what his brother cannot see: that his desire to have a private tutor is motivated by class vanity. The concern to uphold this traditional, elitist method of education is, the Geheimer Rat insists, a symptom of a deep-seated determination on the part of the aristocracy to cling to its pre-eminent social standing and the concomitant structures of inherited power and privilege. The Major's insistence on private education implies, in other words, a refusal to accept the necessity of historical change. The Geheimer Rat draws his brother to admit as much when he asks him what future he envisages for his son. To this the Major expresses his great hope that

> er Major wird, und ein braver Kerl wie ich und dem
> König so redlich dient als ich! (p.6)

This is exactly the answer which the Geheimer Rat has expected. He sees it as proof of his basic conviction that his brother's commitment to private education has nothing to do with pedagogy but is rooted rather in a controlling, though largely unacknowledged, concern to uphold the stable, hierarchical society into which he has been born. Against this the Geheimer Rat sets his passionate belief that the contemporary world is caught up in a process of irreversible change and that no son can simply re live his father's life. The eagerness of the Geheimer Rat to embrace the principle of public education stems from the belief that this alone is in keeping with the spirit of the time and represents one of the main means by which history will create a more humane, equitable and freer world.

The following scene (I,3) lacks the discursive force of its predecessor but it extends Lenz's critical analysis in a particularizing and still more bitterly sardonic way. This scene follows on from the demonstration by the Geheimer Rat of the Major's refusal to accept the necessity of social change. The dramatist's main concern here is to show that such resistance does not just involve a passive ignoring or turning aside, but is fired by powerful aggressive impulses which pervade the most unremarkable, quotidian areas of social intercourse. Every word and gesture of the Major's wife confirms the conviction of the Geheimer Rat that the Bergs' preference for private education stems from a divisive, disparaging vanity. Like her husband the Majorin seems to need the presence of the tutor in her household in order to be vitally, assertively conscious of her standing as an aristocrat. Lenz shows in fact that she is driven by some deep, wordless need to control and even degrade her middle-class tutor before she can feel completely at one with herself. The constant need to subject Läuffer is evident in the way she arranges over his head with his father to cut his salary by half and in her pretence that she does not even remember his name when she gives him the shattering news (p.7). This destructive impulse is even more ominously apparent in her consistent attempts to deny him all possibility of personal choice and judgement. Although she has entrusted her children's education to his care she seems bent on makig him a man without opinion or conviction. It is as if something ceaselessly compels her to destroy Läuffer's intellectual superiority and richer cultural awareness. The force of this vindictive drive breaks into the open in the middle of the scene when the tutor dares to put forward a view about a theatrical performer at odds with that of her aspiring upper-class visitor, Graf Wermuth:

> Merk Er sich, mein Freund! daß Domestiken in Gesellschaften von Standespersonen nicht mitreden. Geh Er auf Sein Zimmer. Wer hat Ihn gefragt? (p.9)

Having been outrageously exploited and mercilessly patronized by the Major's wife Läuffer now finds himself rebuked as an impertinent servant and banished like a wanton child. His humiliation is complete.

In this scene Lenz seems to be revealing a hidden link between the Majorin's urge to undermine the individuality of Läuffer and her husband's hatred of the town school and its potentially warping influence on the minds of impressionable upper-class youths (pp.6f.). In both cases the dramatist exposes an impelling hostility towards other social groups of which neither the Major nor his wife are fully conscious: a will to destroy their claim to rights and standards of their own which might in some way call in question the privileges of the nobility.

In this as in the previous scene it is clear that Lenz's main aim is to present the predicament of Läuffer as the symptom of deep antagonisms pervading contemporary existence but which the characters themselves cannot fully acknowledge. The figure of the tutor is of crucial relevance to the dramatist's socially critical concerns less as the representative of a particular method of education than as a member of an emergent educated, articulate middle-class which has not yet achieved a defined and significant role in the life of contemporary society.

All the various critical impulses expressed in these introductory scenes are gathered up and examined anew in the first scene of the second act (II,1), which forms the climax of this part of the exposition. This is a scene of great ironic probing force which widens the historical scope of Lenz's social exposition and in so doing forces us to re-examine and reassess the attitudes which the dramatist has been studying.

Here again, this time in discussion with Läuffer's father, the Geheimer Rat condemns the motives of upper-class families who employ private tutors. Face to face with the Pastor, however, he goes further and also criticizes the weakness of those highly educated, intellectually aspiring young men who willingly enter into the shaming serfdom of the tutor's existence. His tone is scathing:

> Wer heißt euch Domestiken werden, wenn ihr was gelernt habt, und einem starrköpfischen Edelmann zinsbar werden, der sein Tage von seinen Hausgenossen nichts anders gewohnt war als sklavische Unterwürfigkeit? (p.19).

The Pastor's response to this is just as abrasive, although much more diplomatically expressed. On the one hand, although he is in general very well disposed to his upper-class patrons, he conspicuously refrains from defending their preference for private education. At the same time he also vigorously rejects this sweeping criticism of the young men who, like his son, accept positions as private tutors. Such a criticism, he discreetly implies, is rooted in idealistic preconceptions which do no justice to the great hardship which these young graduates experience (p.15). He seems to be suggesting that the readiness of the Geheimer Rat to condemn the tutors is evidence of that disregarding arrogance which the latter condemns in his brother: that it represents a condescension peculiar to a priveleged caste. By attributing to these hard-pressed, middle-class intellectuals the same degree of choice he himself enjoys he is reducing (the Pastor hints) what is essentially a serious social problem to a matter of individual attitude. The problem, he insists, does not lie with the tutor but with a system which denies adequate opportunities to graduates with a middle-class background. It is revealing that the Geheimer Rat fails completely to see the point of the Pastor's argument, an argument which arises directly out of the latter's actual experience as a young man. The nobleman's impatience with Pastor Läuffer shows that he has not really understood what his interlocutor has been saying, and has not in fact really been listening. His preconceptions remain untouched:

Possen! lernt etwas und seid brave Leut'. Der Staat wird euch nicht lang am Markt stehenlassen. Brave Leut' sind allenthalben zu brauchen... (p.20).

The fact that the Geheimer Rat who is such a consistent and unsparing critic of the prejudices and vanities of his own class should hold such an unthinkingly optimistic view of the organization of society is very remarkable. It is evident that he is unable to recognize the hidden contention which impels the Pastor's defence of tutors like his son - to the effect that their plight stems largely from the refusal of the aristocracy to relinquish their hold on all the positions of genuine social power and standing, those positions through which alone able, aspiring middle-class graduates could play a full, communally beneficial role in the life of contemporary society. The Geheimer Rat leaves no doubt that he regards the predicament of Läuffer and other young men in his position as the result of a lack of personal energy and resolve. This is in keeping with his deepest guiding assumptions. His endeavours as a moralist and pedagogue consistently presuppose that the individual has the power to come to terms with the circumstances in which he is caught up, to transcend them inwardly and do in the end what he knows in himself to be right. He is equally convinced that the creation of a more liberal and just society can be achieved only by the concurring efforts of countless individuals each motivated by a deep personal sense of ideal purpose.

In this crucial scene of social exposition Lenz is primarily concerned to relativize the outlook of the Geheimer Rat. In his earlier discussions with the Major he had appeared as a perceptive, detached *raisonneur* who exposed the disregarding arrogance and egotism of the social group to which he himself belongs. In the course of his confrontation with the Pastor, however, it becomes clear that his response to the behaviour of other social groups is conditioned by his class-identity, by his experience as a member of a privileged, powerful elite, in ways he himself cannot perceive.[2] This is most obvious in his inability to assess the profound sense of insecurity which besets those young middle-class graduates who struggle to find a foothold in the life of society without wealth,

---

[2] Critics have consistently failed to grasp these contradictions in the outlook and behaviour of the Geheimer Rat. Arntzen for example regards him as an essentially rational individual who is incapacitated by his isolation in an irrational world (7, p.89). Butler similarly sees him as 'a man of integrity' who, however, is swept off balance 'in a tide of events' he cannot understand (9, pp.96f.). Guthrie does sense contradictions in the behaviour of the Geheimer Rat but sees these as unintended, as a symptom of Lenz's failure to motivate the character consistently (20, pp.59f.). The revelation of his unacknowledged dependence on his class background is in my view a fundamental aspect of Lenz's socially critical concern and of decisive importance for the motivation of the dramatic crisis.

patronage or the awareness of an inherited social authority. The Pastor, himself of relatively humble origins, intuitively perceives the self-deception underlying the moralistic assurance of his upper-class superior. But his scepticism has obviously been sharpened by his consciousness of the arrogantly dismissive way the Geheimer Rat has destroyed his son's hopes of being appointed to the vacant position at the local school despite his high academic credentials (p.9). The Pastor is surely right in sensing here the self-certainty of a man so versed in the exercise of power that he has lost the capacity to question his own judgements or to consider sympathetically how his actions impinge upon the lives of others. The Geheimer Rat is well able to criticize the general attitudes of his class but cannot conceive that his own outlook and responses may be affected by the same group assumptions. He can see the self-deception of the Pastor as the latter struggles to rationalize his own selfish impulses, but he observes this with the dispassionate critical superiority of one not himself susceptible to moral confusion or prejudice.

Exposition (iii): Family Conflict and Estrangement

The position of Läuffer, the middle-class intellectual held at bay by his exploiting aristocratic superiors, is a central focus of Lenz's socially critical concern. Over the years commentators have repeatedly stressed the historical importance of the playwright's openly polemical, combative portrayal of class-relations in *Der Hofmeister*, and there is no doubt that this does represent a basic and strikingly controversial aspect of Lenz's conception (27, pp.166ff.). By contrast, however, critics have shown little concerted interest in his view of family relations in the play which, it seems to me, is an equally radical and provocative area of his critical preoccupation. It is true of course, as I have already stressed, that these two searching critical impulses constantly overlap and interpenetrate. Lenz made consistent efforts to show the life of the family as impelled by the momentum of socio-historical forces, to present it in fact as the microcosm of collective existence. He was consciously in revolt against the tendency of many playwrights in the previous generation to portray the world of the family as a realm of timeless emotion and moral aspiration which transcended the relativizing influence of contingent social circumstances (*35*, pp.65ff.). Despite this, however, Lenz does seem to have sensed in the life of the family the working of some force of compulsion which was essentially inscrutable. In familial loyalties and conflicts he seemed to feel the power of archaic instinct and emotion before which the rational individual was helpless and which he experienced as a kind of fateful force. There is something obsessive in his concern with family relationships as if they were for him a constant source of powerful elusive mystery which demanded ceaseless imaginative exploration.

In *Der Hofmeister* the dramatist sees his characters as doubly exposed and doubly constrained. He is constantly aware, on the one hand, of their subjection to the impersonal processes of a divided, hostile society. But he also sees his characters as bound by the inexorable emotional pressures of domestic existence. He seeks constantly to show the peculiar helplessness of the individual driven into conflict with those closest to him, a conflict he does not seek and never fully understands. In this too Lenz recognizes a kind of victimization which is equally irreversible and potentially just as destructive. In all the families presented in *Der Hofmeister* he shows a tendency to division and deep disharmony, the final causes of which he is unable to penetrate. In particular Lenz is concerned in every case to lay bare a fundamental discrepancy between the self-awareness of the parent, the way he sees himself, his position in the world, and the basic emotional needs of his child. The dramatist is driven over and over again to examine this discrepancy, to probe it as a symptom of an alienation between parent and child in which each confronts the other as a stranger, each trapped in the momentum of his own existence and cut off from the mind and the heart of the other.

This distinctive sense of the two-fold entrapment of the individual pervades the opening scene of *Der Hofmeister*. The fierce sense of resentment impelling Läuffer's reflections here as we have seen, does not stem solely from his experience of exploitation and humiliation at the hands of his upper-class-employers, however distressing this has proved. His anger is directed in the first place at his own father, who in his comfortable and respected position as Pastor refuses to recognize his plight and intervene on his behalf. It is quite clear that Läuffer regards the Major, the Geheimer Rat and probably also his professors at the University as having abused and denigrated him. The indifference of his father, however, represents for Läuffer the ultimate act of betrayal. The Pastor in his complacent, untouched self-concern seeks solely (the tutor feels) to protect his savings, the ease and security of his own life, and abandons him to shame and hopelessness. Läuffer's tearing bitterness is heightened by what he sees as the hypocritical attempts of his father to mask from himself the depths of his own egoism. The Pastor's proclaimed doubts about his son's intellectual capacities are nothing more (the tutor insists) than a vain attempt to justify to himself a materialism and self-regard he refuses to admit.

The indignant, frustrated tutor is uncompromising in his sweeping indictment of his father. The dramatist, however, enables the spectator to see beyond the remorseless judgements of the son and to sense ambiguities in the experience of the Pastor to which the tutor in his resentment is blind. In the opening scene of the second act Lenz in fact is intent on revealing to us a man whom the son does not know and will probably never know. It becomes quite evident here that the Pastor is proud of his son and indignant that he should have been financially exploited in such a ruthless way:

> Aber bedenken Sie doch: nichts mehr als hundert Dukaten; hundert arme Dukätchen; und dreihundert hatt' er ihm doch im ersten Jahr versprochen: aber beim Schluß desselben nur hundertundvierzig ausgezahlt, jetzt, beim Beschluß des zweiten, da doch die Arbeit meines Sohnes immer zunimmt, zahlt' er ihm hundert, und nun beim Anfang des dritten wird ihm auch das zuviel. — Das ist wider alle Billigkeit! Verzeihn Sie mir.
> (p.17)

It is also obvious that he is deeply moved by his son's predicament, so deeply indeed that he forces himself to beg the Geheimer Rat to intercede with his brother on the tutor's behalf (p.19).

But despite this the Pastor is still unwilling to give his son the money he needs to embark on an academic career. This refusal seems at first sight all the more puzzling as the Pastor himself has undergone the same draining experience of frustration and entrapment which now besets his son. He too has known the bondage of a life of drudgery, without recognition or hope of release (p.19). Only marriage to a woman of wealth freed him from this empty existence and enabled him to enter a new life in the service of the Church. He, if anyone, Lenz suggests, must be able to feel what his son is suffering and recognize the liberating power of money. Despite this, however, the Pastor is unable to make the sacrificial gesture which his son demands. The fact that his son's experience is so similar to what he himself underwent as a young man serves in the end rather to deter and inhibit his response in a way he himself cannot grasp. It is as if his awareness of his own unexpected deliverance had exposed him to a deep irrational fear of the uncertainty of things and the need to avoid any action which might jeopardize the stability of his present existence. For all his apparent prosperity he seems constrained by a compulsive hidden dread which prevents him from reaching out to rescue his son from his deepening despair. The events in the Pastor's own life which might seem to open him to his son's experience have the effect of separating father and son, of estranging them from one another with a force that can never be checked.

Lenz shows the same process of mutual estrangement at work in the household of the Major. He appears throughout as a deeply conservative officer, proud of his military rank and social standing and very conscious of his position as head of the family. At the same time he is clearly troubled by the sense of his inadequacy in his dealings with his sexually dominant, aggressive wife. Every relationship in the Berg family is profoundly affected by this primary antagonism between husband and wife. The Major's frenetic and seemingly ruthless determination to control every aspect of his son's development and make his life the effective replica of his own, is fired, Lenz suggests, by the Major's constant need to compensate for his loss of authority in his relationship with his wife. This becomes clear when he directs Läuffer to treat his daughter with a sensitivity and deference quite inapproprate to the education of his son:

> Meine Frau macht mir bittre Tage genug: sie will alleweil herrschen, und weil sie mehr List und Verstand hat als ich. Und der Sohn, das ist ihr Liebling; den will sie nach ihrer Methode erziehen; fein säuberlich mit dem Knaben Absalom, und da wird denn einmal so ein Galgenstrick draus, der nicht Gott, nicht Menschen was nutz ist. — Das will ich nicht haben. — Sobald er was tut, oder was versieht, oder hat seinen Lex nicht gelernt, sag Er's mir nur, und der lebendige Teufel soll dreinfahren. — Aber mit der Tochter nehm Er sich in acht; die Frau wird Ihm schon zureden, daß Er ihr scharf begegnen soll. Sie kann sie nicht leiden, das weiß ich; aber wo ich das Geringste merke. Ich bin Herr vom Hause, muß Er wissen, und wer meiner Tochter zu nahe kommt... (p.12)

His attempts to govern his son reflect an unadmitted urge to heighten his self-esteem and demonstrate his power to his disdainful, embittered spouse. This has the effect, however, of trapping all the members of the family in a deepening cycle of hostility. The more harshly the Major attempts to repress what he sees as rebellious tendencies in his son's behaviour, the more devious and far-reaching the boy's defiance seems to become; as the boy grows increasingly intractable in his father's eyes, so the ferocity of the punishments rained down upon him increases (p.10ff.). The attempts of the Majorin to intercede on her son's behalf contrive only to heighten the tensions. Her intrusions inevitably appear to her husband as part of an involved conspiracy to undermine his authority and thus drive him the more violently to re-assert his paternal control (p.39).

Lenz also makes very clear that it is the Major's unhappy marriage which drives him into his increasingly obsessional and manipulative relationship with his daughter Gustchen. In his love for her he seeks blindly to make good the draining emptiness of his existence. He sees her existence as set apart from that of all other beings, and senses that it is through her and her alone that his life can find fulfilment:

> Alle Tage ist sie in meinem Abendgebet und Morgengebet und in meinem Tischgebet und alles in allem, und wenn Gott mir die Gnade tun wollte, daß ich sie noch vor meinem Ende mit einem General oder Staatsminister vom ersten Range versorgt sähe - denn keinen andern soll sie sein Lebtage bekommen -, so wollt' ich gern ein zehn Jahr' eher sterben. (p.12f.)

Here, as throughout the play, Lenz seems to be pointing up the gap between the power of the Major's paternal feelings and the distorted form in which they find expression. Although his love for his daughter is profound and charges his whole existence, it tends to confuse or deform his day-to-day contact with her. His love drives him constantly back on himself, into a realm of reflection and fantasy in which he is able to promote her happiness and success in an ideal future. This, however, has the effect of separating him more and more from the vulnerable adolescent girl before him (pp.11f.). Intimidated by his grandiose dreams Gustchen recoils from her father and hides her deepest feelings from him. As the weeks go by he loses touch more and more with the one person he really loves (pp.34f.). It is no accident that it is not the Major but the Geheimer Rat who discovers her hidden passion for her cousin, Fritz. For this is a relationship which for her father must not and indeed cannot exist.

It is, however, the behaviour of the Geheimer Rat as a parent that assumes greatest prominence in Lenz's expository scheme. His dealings with his son and niece are of crucial importance to the dramatist's socially critical purpose and are subjected to extended analytical scrutiny. They also have, as Lenz makes very clear, a decisive impact on the subsequent development of the dramatic action.

We have repeatedly noted the important function of the Geheimer Rat as a spokesman of the dramatist's polemical concerns and in particular of his attempts to expose the inadequacies of other parents in the play. It is above all the Geheimer Rat who shows up the force of prejudice and class-aggression in the household of his brother, the Major, and who lays bare the contradictions in the attitude of Pastor Läuffer towards his son. But this figure also fulfils another equally important diagnostic function. The Geheimer Rat is the only figure in the play who puts forward a progressive theoretical view of education. He rejects the authoritarian assumptions which his brother (and probably also Pastor Läuffer) accepts unthinkingly, and which govern accepted conceptions of the educative process in contemporary society. He sees pedagogy not as a repressive system of control, of the imposition of fixed standards and goals, but rather as a process of drawing out and fostering the creative impulses inherent in the individuality of the child. The precondition of all valid educational methods, as the Geheimer Rat insists, is the acknowledgement of the uniqueness of the pupil and of his right to develop in accordance with the intrinsic laws of his own being. For him freedom is the precondition of all genuine learning and teaching. He makes this clear to the perplexed Pastor:

> Freiheit ist das Element des Menschen wie das Wasser
> des Fisches, und ein Mensch, der sich der Freiheit
> begibt, vergiftet die edelsten Geister seines Bluts,
> erstickt seine süßesten Freuden des Lebens in der Blüte
> und ermordet sich selbst. (p.18)

Here the Geheimer Rat appears as the proponent of a liberal, forward-looking conception of education which, as we know from Lenz's other writings, were close to his heart (*39*, p.106). There can be no doubt that the dramatist expects us to accept these views as

both enlightened and humane and to use them as a standard to judge
the attitudes of the other figures.

To this extent, it seems, the Geheimer Rat functions as the
agent of Lenz's polemic purpose. However, the dramatist is intent on
setting his presentation of the Geheimer Rat as an enlightened
educational theorist and moralist against that of his behaviour as a
practising parent aware of his inalienable responsibility for the moral
and material welfare of his children. Lenz asserts this provocative
incongruity most powerfully in the final scene of the opening act
(I,6), one of the decisive turning-points of the dramatic development.

In this scene the Geheimer Rat quite unexpectedly comes upon
his son, Fritz, and his niece, Gustchen, declaring their undying love
for one another on bended knee. He is completely taken aback by
this spectacle and obviously feels that this relationship which has
flourished in secret and without his consent, entails a sharp breach of
his paternal authority. Lenz emphasizes the importance of the
response to the Geheimer Rat to this sudden crisis and explores it in
great detail and from different points of view. He makes it clear that
this response must inevitably have a decisive impact on the lives of
the two young lovers. At the same time he stresses its immense
diagnostic significance: its power to reveal powerful impulses in the
make-up of the Geheimer Rat which in the normal continuum of
day-to-day existence remain undisclosed.

Lenz stresses the spontaneous and seemingly quite involuntary
reaction of the Geheimer Rat to this unexpected situation. His first
unthinking impulse is to reassert his parental control. He does so,
however, in a peculiarly destructive way: by ridiculing the love
which Fritz and Gustchen have just declared. He cruelly disparages
their feelings for each other as childish and their impassioned vows
as empty, deluded and insincere:

> Pfui, ich glaubt' einen vernünftigern Sohn zu haben. Das
> macht dich gleich ein Jahr jünger und macht, daß du
> länger auf der Schule bleiben mußt. Und Sie, Gustchen,
> auch Ihnen muß ich sagen, daß es sich für Ihr Alter gar
> nicht mehr schickt, so kindisch zu tun. Was sind das für

Romane, die Sie da spielen? Was für Eide, die Sie da
schwören, und die ihr doch alle beide so gewiß brechen
werdet, als ich itzt mit euch rede. Meint ihr, ihr seid in
den Jahren, Eide zu tun, oder meint ihr, ein Eid sei ein
Kinderspiel, wie es das Versteckspiel oder die blinde
Kuh ist? (p.15)

He then procedes to impose very harsh conditions on the future
conduct of their relationship. He decrees that henceforth they may
not meet in private and that when Fritz is at university in Halle their
letters must be open to his inspection. He also makes clear that any
attempt at defying his authority on the part of the lovers will be met
with very severe punishment - Fritz will be conscripted into the army
and Gustchen placed in a convent for an indefinite period.

The underlying thrust of these measures is not to regulate the
relationship between the two young people, as the Geheimer Rat
claims, but to destroy it. Whether he admits it or not his real aim is
to subvert this anarchic adolescent passion, but to do so in a way
which will make the lovers themselves feel responsible for its
demise.

Lenz is concerned to emphasize the discrepancy between the
repressive severity of these measures and the principles of liberal
individualism which the Geheimer Rat likes to proclaim. The man
who eloquently proclaims the power of choice as the basis of all
genuine human growth is here effectively depriving the lovers of the
possibility of free emotional development in accordance with their
own impelling longings. His decisions, however he attempts to
justify them, are aimed at reducing Fritz and Gustchen to a state of
humiliated submission, and he seeks to achieve this with a ruthless
efficiency which his militaristic brother would envy. What is most
noticeable throughout is that the Geheimer Rat makes very little
effort to enter sympathetically into this relationship he condemns, to
see it from the point of view of the lovers themselves. As a result he
is quite unable to sense the impact which his intervention will have
upon them. The immediacy and force of his reaction indicates how
deeply this love-affair affronts his sense of propriety, of how things

should be. The behaviour of his son seems to defy his view of the way in which an upper-class young man about to leave home and enter the world on his own account should conduct himself. In so doing it appears to the Geheimer Rat to represent a serious challenge to himself and his authority as a father.

The Geheimer Rat does not, however, try to articulate any of this to himself. Indeed, as Lenz sardonically suggests, he cannot do so as this would seriously infringe his cherished image of himself as a champion of personal liberty and self-determination.

Lenz points up this contradiction in order to lay bare the profound tensions in the outlook of the Geheimer Rat which he himself is unable to confront. In his authoritarian treatment of his son, as also in his high-handed disparagement of Läuffer, the dramatist is exposing an imperiousness, a fierce disregarding arrogance, which operates beyond the reach of his conscious self-awareness. Taken off guard by this sudden crisis his reactions are shaped by tendencies very similar to those he condemns in the Major and in the latter's wife. These run directly counter to the desire of the Geheimer Rat to see himself as a rational, liberal individual who lives by ethical principles which transcend all group-prejudice and narrow egoistical concerns.

From the moment the Geheimer Rat discovers Fritz's passion for Gustchen father and son confront each other as adversaries, although neither would describe their relationship in these terms. The overwhelming concern of the Geheimer Rat to re-assert his authority seems to destroy his sensitivity to the youth's feelings. Although he is certainly convinced he is acting in his son's best long-term interests he makes no attempt to put himself in Fritz's position or even to ask himself how the severity of his attitude will affect his son at this crucial stage in his life. His view of the situation, as Lenz repeatedly emphasizes, remains rigidly egocentric and strangely unfeeling, and as a consequence it changes the relationship between father and son in a fundamental and seemingly irreversible way. When Fritz goes out into the adult world of the university in Halle, he leaves without the paternal blessing and support he had taken for granted as a child.

In the lives of all these families (and also, as we shall see, in that of Fritz's friend, Pätus) Lenz traces the same seemingly irresistible process of mutual disconnection and conflict. He exposes in each case an opposition between the outlook and will of the parent and the inner imperatives of the child's life, an opposition which develops implacably, it seems, and with a force neither is able to foresee or control. In *Der Hofmeister* the dramatist sees all those who experience familial antagonisms as victimized and depleted. None of them are able to communicate the fear and anguish which overtakes them, much less to discuss the process through which they come into conflict with them they love.

Lenz recognized that in exploring the disruptions of family existence he was taking over some of the most basic concerns of the classical tragic tradition. Within the narrow compass of his comic form he saw himself as probing by realistic empirical means kinds of conflict and predicament which were potentially timeless and could still exercise great power over the responding imagination. Lenz was certainly concerned to exploit this tragic sense of the mysterious and irreducible nature of familial antagonism and to assimilate it to his innovative conception of comedy as a disparate, encompassing dramatic form (*35*, pp.65ff.).

The exposition in *Der Hofmeister* is informed by a tense discordant energy which makes it seem strangely unresolved but which also lends it an ambiguous questioning power all its own. Lenz's imagination is fired by a strong analytical will to grasp the determinants which shape the life of the individual and to show their working as a closed, accountable process of causality. He seems intent, in other words, on reducing the world of the play to an interlocking network of socio-historical forces which can be analysed by empirical means.

At the same time the dramatist is also driven to evoke hidden powers of instinct and intuition in the dramatic characters which he seems unable to relate fully to the operation of environmental forces. In the everyday domestic world Lenz senses irrational forces at work which resist the pragmatic ways of seeing and assessing that seem to govern other aspects of his dramatic conception. His imagination seems to embrace conflicting modes of perception and to counterpose incongruous perspectives. As a social analyst he is concerned to explore the dependence of the dramatis personae on the conditions of contemporary society. At times, however, he also seeks to evoke a sense of the exposure of the individual as inherent in the conditions of life itself, as existentially given, and as such capable, potentially at least, of tragic presentation.

Development

The reactions of the Geheimer Rat on discovering the secret love-affair between Fritz and Gustchen form, as we have seen, a significant focus of Lenz's expository concern. The dramatist is also concerned to stress the crucial impact of the intervention of the Geheimer Rat on the unfolding of the dramatic action. As the plot develops it becomes clear how deeply his decisions affect the lives of the two young lovers and also obliquely, though just as significantly, that of Läuffer, the stranded tutor.

It is, of course, true that Fritz and Gustchen had already accepted the fact that his departure for Halle would bring a lengthy and painful separation. Nonetheless, the very harsh conditions which his father imposes on their continuing relationship does change the situation substantially. The insistence of the Geheimer Rat that they should submit to a long, unbroken period apart during which they should have no private correspondence, denies them the possibility of living through this painful time of separation as a couple, as lovers united in a shared sense of loss and longing (pp.16f., 70). Each has to confront his isolation alone, insecure, deeply apprehensive and deprived of emotional support. Fritz goes off to university (I have suggested) as a young man who has in a real sense lost the father he has known, but he also leaves cut off from Gustchen in a way he had not anticipated.

The debilitating effects of this situation on Fritz are soon very obvious (p.24f.). After a year in Halle he has had no news from home and still lives from day to day in a state of draining, edgy anxiety. The fact that he is unable to write directly to Gustchen seems in particular to have demoralized him and driven him into a state of uneasy inertia. Pätus remarks:

> Ich weiß nicht, wie du auch bist; ein Jahr in Halle und noch mit keinem Mädchen gesprochen: das muß melancholisch machen; es kann nicht anders sein. Warte, du mußt mir hier einziehen, daß du lustig wirst. (p.25)

Although, as his friends have noticed, he has not as much as looked at another girl, and Gustchen is constantly in his thoughts, some deep-seated sense of resentment or frustration has prevented him from writing home. This, inevitably, has had the effect of heightening further his pervasive feeling of disorientated impotence.

Fritz's condition is aggravated by another great source of anxiety: his concern for Pätus, his closest friend from home. He is devoted to Pätus and feels driven to make up for the erratic, often brutal treatment which the latter suffers at the hand of a heartless, tyrannical father who denies him not just paternal love but also the steady financial support he needs to pursue his studies (pp.25ff.).[3] So great is Fritz's commitment to his childhood friend that he is ready to stand guarantor for his steadily rising debts and in fact, inevitably it seems, ends up in prison (pp.35ff.). The shattering force of this experience, coinciding as it does with his thwarted longing for Gustchen, thrusts Fritz into a disabling state of dejection which erodes his normal vitality and confidence.

Gustchen, meanwhile, still in her parents' home in Heidelbrunn is also undergoing her own experience of entrapment. She lives from day to day, as she tells Läuffer, cut off from girls of her own age by the snobbery of her parents, resented by her 'barbaric' mother, and ignored by her increasingly morose and withdrawn father (p.31). She sees herself as a girl imprisoned in a pointless existence: 'von der

---

[3] The predicament of Pätus closely reflects Lenz's own experience as a student in Königsberg (*10*, pp.72ff.). This probably explains the dramatist's generally very sympathetic portrayal of a character who often seems self-indulgent and erratic. It also explains Lenz's very positive view of Fritz's unwavering loyalty to his childhood friend.

ganzen Welt, von ihrer ganzen Familie gehaßt, verachtet, ausgespien'
(p.32).

Deprived of all news of Fritz, and fearing the worst, Gustchen
drifts more and more into a world of melancholy imaginings. This
serves only to estrange her further from those around her and to
heighten her sense of forsakenness. Gradually she falls prey to a
seeping, depressed listlessness, which, as even the Major is forced to
see, is seriously undermining her health (p.39).

For Läuffer too, things have gone from bad to worse. With the
passing of the months he sees his conditions of service deteriorate
steadily and the hopes which had animated him in earlier days begin
to fade like an empty dream. During his involuntarily prolonged stay
in the Major's household his salary has been progressively reduced
without discussion from the 300 ducats originally promised him to a
mere 60 after Fritz's departure (p.22), and finally to a humiliating 40
ducats on which, he fears, he will not be able to survive (p.32). On
top of this he feels constantly abased by the insistence of the Majorin
that he must always eat with the servants whenever she is
entertaining guests (p.22). Läuffer is equally incensed by the fact
that the Major should blithely break his promise to give the tutor a
horse so that he could make regular trips to Königsberg (p.22). The
cumulative effect of all this has been overwhelming. The more his
sense of shame and frustration has deepened, the more trapped he
has felt at Heidelbrunn and the less able to conceive of a new
fulfilling existence.

Lenz seems intent on showing that, despite all the obvious
differences, the position of Läuffer is fundamentally similar to that
of Gustchen. Both are devoured by a bitter thwarted longing, both
dream of a release which has the sole effect of alienating them the
more deeply from the real circumstances which imprison them. Yet
although their sufferings are so alike they remain apart. For all that
they are in daily intimate contact they remain in a real sense
strangers to one another. The dramatist shows how each remains
clenched in his own draining grief which he cannot adequately
express and which in the end cuts him off from the other's suffering.

Lenz emphasizes the mutual inner separation of Läuffer and Gustchen, for it is this, paradoxically, which impels the brief but fateful sexual encounter between them. Their blundering, uneasy coming together is presented as a pitiful travesty of a freeing passionate union. It is devoid not just of all erotic yearning but almost, it seems, of urgent sexual desire. Both young people are driven rather by a blind compulsive search for release, for an escape from a suffocating sense of oppression. The dramatist emphasizes the essentially illusory, evasive nature of this union by showing that neither of the 'lovers' is able to face the reality of the other, that each gives himself in the grip of fantasies which obscure and even suspend the identity of the other. Gustchen yields to her tutor in the trance-like certainty that the man before her is in fact Fritz, her 'göttlicher Romeo' who has returned from afar to make her his own (p.32). Läuffer for his part takes the crucial step seized by a heroic vision of himself as Abelard, the tragic lover who defies the world and the terrible retribution it will visit upon him.

In his sardonic presentation of this sad and passionless seduction Lenz is stressing above all its peculiarly hesitant half-heartedness. It is an act which fails to evoke any sense of loyalty or commitment in the two participants. If there is any doubt at all about this it is dispelled the moment the lovers' guilty secret is discovered. They flee as in blind panic, but separately and in different directions (pp.40f.). Läuffer finds sanctuary with Wenzeslaus, an eccentric but courageous teacher in a nearby village. Gustchen takes refuge with a blind beggar-woman in the depths of the forest (pp.52f.).

The flights of Gustchen and Läuffer from Heidelbrunn have the effect of fragmenting the action of the play so severely as to change its essential formal character. In the opening act all the protagonists are grouped together in and around Heidelbrunn and are in potential day-to-day contact with one another. When Fritz begins his new life as a student in Halle (II,3) the action splits into two clear parallel strands of development which are independent of each other and take place in separate locations far apart. Now with Gustchen and Läuffer (each unbeknown to the other) finding refuge in quite different places (III,2), the scene swings constantly, and sometimes disconcertingly, back and forth between four diverse settings. The action now overtly assumes the form of single separate movements which, as far as we can judge, unfold roughly simultaneously, but which appear as quite unrelated.

This fragmentation expresses in powerfully scenic form the mutual disconnection of the dramatic figures. All the parents are now separated from their children, ignorant of their whereabouts and of their state of wellbeing. The children appear as isolated in an even more extreme way: as exiled from home and family and cut off from one another. All the characters are deeply anxious about Gustchen. The Major is driven month after month to mount constant frenetic searches for her which seem quite unavailing (pp.50f.). Läuffer and Fritz in their different situations and in their different ways also become increasingly apprehensive about her. Like her father neither has any idea where she is or in what state she may be (pp.63f., 69ff.). Gustchen meanwhile, conscious of being cut off from the ordered world she once knew by the shame of being an unmarried mother falls victim to deepening apprehension and hopelessness. Consumed by remorse she thinks constantly of her father while her memories of Fritz only serve to heighten her despair (pp.52f.).

Each character, trapped in his own condition of untouchable isolation, appears more and more as a separate focus of action. Each, Lenz shows, is forced in on himself, driven to confront alone every passing rumour, and increasingly vulnerable to the morbid anxieties which beset his imagination. All the protagonists, whatever their circumstances, appear as exposed, isolated and helpless. This situation, Lenz forces us to realize, is charged with catastrophic possibilities.

Things do indeed deteriorate steadily. Step by step the three young protagonists move inexorably, it seems, towards disaster. Gustchen, in the grip of devouring feelings of remorse, dreams of her stricken father: 'Sein Bild, o sein Bild steht mir immer vor den Augen! Er ist tot, ja tot — und für Gram um mich'... (p.56).

In despair she decides to make good her terrible guilt in the only way she can — by taking her own life. She goes to the lake and throws herself in.

Shortly after this Läuffer, as chance would have it, happens to meet Marthe, carrying a baby. She informs him that the child is now an orphan; a workman has told her that her mother has drowned herself (pp.63f.). Läuffer takes the baby in his arms and is seized at once by the terrifying conviction that this is his child, that it is Gustchen who has committed suicide and that he is responsible for everything. He falls into a dead faint. The next time he appears he tells Wenzeslaus that, overwhelmed by guilt and despair, he has castrated himself (pp.66f.). However, far from assuaging his remorse and opening up a new life he fears that his wound will kill him. Now that it is too late Läuffer bitterly regrets his impulsive and futile action.

Fritz, meanwhile, who is far away from these events in Leipzig, also hears that Gustchen is dead. A letter from the conniving Seiffenblase informs him that she was seduced by her tutor and had become so unhinged by the experience that she has killed herself (pp.69f.). Fritz, like Läuffer, is seized by an overwhelming awareness of his guilt. He, and he alone, is responsible: 'Ich bin ein Bösewicht: ich bin schuld an ihrem Tode' (pp.70f.).

Far from home and unable to return, he seems to slip deeper and deeper into a remorse-ridden, helpless depression.

One after the other Gustchen, Fritz and Läuffer succumb to an overwhelming awareness of guilt that in each case is precipitated by the conviction that a catastrophe has taken place for which they are to blame. Lenz presents this experience in a sharply ironic way: the spectator knows that Gustchen is not, in fact, dead and that the deluded belief that she is stems from flimsy and unsupported evidence. The dramatist is forcing us to recognize the gap between what the characters believe and feel and the actual situation in which they find themselves. However devastating the experience of remorse which possesses them, it is irrelevant to what has actually happened and from this point of view seems absurd. Lenz is also suggesting, however, that this is only part of a vaster and more fundamental absurdity. The most ludicrous aspect of this experience of guilt is not that it arises out of a misapprehension of the facts but rather that it reveals the preconditioned readiness of the figures to assume responsibility for events which, even if they had actually taken place, lay far beyond their control. In succumbing to these compulsive feelings of remorse they are deceived not just by their credulousness in a particular situation but by their basic inability to grasp the nature of their existence as determined, driven beings in a contingent world.

This common experience of guilt which possesses the three youthful protagonists acquires a clinching symptomatic significance in Lenz's presentation of the dramatic developments. It reveals a contradiction between the empirical forces shaping the movement of the plot and the self-awareness of the characters who are to a large extent the vehicles of these forces. The dramatist is pointing up the fundamental rift between the sensibility of individuals conditioned from birth to regard themselves as free, responsible agents and the reality of lives controlled by the impersonal momentum of socio-historical processes. The surrender of Gustchen, Läuffer and Fritz to the disintegrating power of remorse reveals a kind of inner dependence, of moral constriction, so severe that it undermines their effective agency as moral subjects.

At this point in the dramatic action Lenz, it would seem, is intent on realizing the conception of a new kind of radical social drama. His experimental initiative here seems strikingly original and has, I believe, considerable historical importance. It is, in fact, not going too far to claim that in *Der Hofmeister* he is probing the possibilities of a new kind of dramatic form impelled by a harsh sceptical awareness of the exposure of the individual in a prepotent, alien society. Seen from this point of view Lenz seems to be taking the first decisive steps towards new rigorous kinds of realism in the drama which, as we can see looking back, anticipate the main developments in the genre throughout the 19th century.

Resolution

Contrary to all expectations, however, the crises besetting the different protagonists do not lead to catastrophe. In every case events unfold in a way which is quite unpredictable and which enables the characters to find rescue and new hope.

At the very moment when Gustchen tries to drown herself her father (who has been searching for her in vain for over a year) happens to be passing by and manages to save her (pp.56f.).

Fritz too in his very different circumstances is also rescued unexpectedly from his deepening hopelessness. The report of Gustchen's death fills him with a terrible anxiety which, he knows, he can only resolve at home. He recognizes that, in debt as he is and without hope of financial relief in the near future, this is impossible (p.71). At this time of draining fear and depression Pätus has a stupendous win on the lottery, a win so immense that both he and Fritz are able to pay off all their debts at a stroke and journey home in regal comfort. Pätus senses in this great piece of good luck the working of a beneficent fate and it is certainly true that from this point on the fortunes of both friends miraculously improve. Fritz's meeting with his father releases a wealth of spontaneous good will, a mutual longing for reconciliation which sweeps away all past divisions (pp.85ff.). He eagerly renews his vow of undying love to Gustchen and embraces her child as his own. His happiness is complete: 'O was hab ich von einer solchen Frau anders zu gewarten als einen Himmel?' (p.86).

At the same time Pätus is also reconciled with his father and united with the girl he loves, Jungfer Rehaar. In his happiness he expresses a sense of sheer joy which passes all understanding: 'Bin ich so glücklich? Oder ist's nur ein Traum? Ein Rausch — Eine Bezauberung?' (p.83).

In his lonely anguish Läuffer too experiences a deliverance seemingly just as miraculous. In the third-last scene of the play Lise, a peasant girl, of whom the spectator knows nothing at all, appears at Läuffer's door (p.77). It turns out that she has been a pupil of his, although he has scarcely been aware of her existence. Now, however, Läuffer senses in her a mysterious power of beauty and goodness so strong that he is forced to his knees in awe. Lise, he knows with absolute assurance, can heal him and give direction and meaning to his stricken existence (p.79). She, for her part, feels so drawn to her teacher, so enraptured by his academic and spiritual stature, that she is quite unperturbed by his confession that he has castrated himself. She declares simply that theirs will be a higher order of love which surpasses 'tierische Triebe', a love both pure and emotionally intense (pp.78f.).

The conclusion of the play thus brings general reconciliation and the happiness of all the protagonists. This happy ending has a starkly disconcerting quality.[4] It obviously perplexed Lenz's contemporaries profoundly. The very first discussions of the play were on the whole remarkably favourable but it is clear that reviewers did not know what to make of an ending so arbitrarily contrived and unexpected. Well-known critics like Christian Schubart, Gottlob Heyne and Christoph Martin Wieland all praised the vigour of Lenz's realism and the energy of the dramatic development but were disturbed by the feeling that the comic resolution was out of keeping with the rest of the play (*53*, pp.99ff.). The ambivalent response of the anonymous reviewer in the *Beytrag zum Reichs-Postreuther* in 1774 was characteristic of many. On the one hand he was full of praise for Lenz's creative abilities and found in *Der Hofmeister* 'viel Spuren eines großen Genies'. At the same time, however, he criticized the playwright's failure to create a unified, coherently motivated action:

> Es kommen überdieß in dieser Comedie so viel Vorfälle, die im geringsten nicht präparirt sind, von welchen man nicht weiß, wie sie zur Würklichkeit kommen, so viel übel zusammenhängende Scenen ... (*6*, pp.63ff.).

In this, as in several other discussions of the play, we can see how insensitive critics in the 1770s were to the fundamentally ironical, parodistic impulse of Lenz's comic perception. They saw

---

[4] Osborne emphasizes the destruction of the illusion here and quotes Lenz's own criticism of Quincey's failure in *L'Honnête criminel* to touch the readers' emotions. The senses here, Lenz complains, have been 'durch ungereimte Erscheinungen, wie in einem Schattenspiel, mehr befremdet und betäubt als gerührt' (*39*, p.116).

him as simply failing to sustain the innovative, searching energy of the play's early sections, as subsiding into convention because he lacked the inventive energy to achieve an ending appropriate to his essentially realistic conception. Lenz must have been both hurt and ruefully amused by these criticisms. To be accused of being negligent and banal when he had worked so hard to appear to be just that, must have been an odd and galling experience.

Lenz was most certainly aware of the dislocation in the dramatic development and probably intended precisely that disconcerting, estranging impact which contemporary reviewers felt. We can see that he consistently emphasizes the incoherence and the improbability of the plot and lays bare the overt fraudulence of the resolution which it precipitates.

Lenz seems to take a perverse pleasure in stressing that his characters are saved by chance and by chance alone: that it is only a freakish concatenation of circumstances which brings them back from the edge of irrevocable disaster. Pätus' massive win on the lottery is by its very nature a happy fluke, but it is no more unlikely than the fact that the itinerant Major should happen to be passing by at the very second Gustchen leaps into the water. Perhaps neither is as improbable, however, as the emergence ex nihilo of the beautiful peasant girl who in her mystical quest for spiritual, sublimated love throws herself passionately at the mutilated Läuffer. Lenz acknowledges that each of these developments is in itself implausible to the point of complete absurdity.

But he is not content with this. He makes it clear that only the impeccable (though quite accidental) confluence of them all allows the deliverance of the three youthful protagonists and probably of their parents as well. And this, the dramatist is insisting, is both incredible and ludicrous. He seems, in other words, to be drawing ironic attention to his own basic failure as a playwright to motivate the comic resolution. He has completely failed (he seems to admit) to derive the happy ending from the tensions he reveals in the earlier parts of the play, and has had to bring it about by means of an arbitrary and violently improbable manipulation of developments.

In highlighting this basic incongruity between exposition and comic finale Lenz seems to be stressing disingenuously his own inadequacies as a dramatist, in particular his inability to sustain the thrust of his initial analytical conception. He has failed (or so he seems to claim) to carry through the task he set himself: to pursue his analysis of the fundamental antagonisms of contemporary society to their logical, and that means catastrophic, 'tragic' conclusion. Instead he has retreated into a realm of conventional comic illusion in which conflicts can be painlessly resolved, individuals effortlessly reunited and enabled to begin life anew. The playwright announces this move from the contradictions of the real world of society to the fictitious, escapist realm of the theatre by emphasizing that all the devices he uses to bypass the intensifying crises and re-direct the action towards a happy outcome, are the staple instruments of comedy, hallowed by the venerable traditions of the genre.[5] Comedy, Lenz seems to claim in mock innocence, is a mode which (more than any other dramatic form) thrives on violent reversals of fortune and the unpredictability of circumstance, a mode which has always flouted normal laws of probability and verisimilitude. Has he not then, as a writer of comedy, the right to use to the full the panoply of contrivance which the traditions of the genre make available to him and which the audience in any case certainly expect — the accidents, coincidences, the unaccountable intrusions which make for an exhilarating, popular theatrical spectacle? Nevertheless, despite all such tongue-in-cheek special pleading Lenz was certainly aware that given the analytical, socially critical conception of *Der Hofmeister* the comic resolution must inevitably appear as implausible, irrelevant and, above all, false.

Lenz, however, is not simply concerned to discredit the conciliatory ending of the play from the point of view of its

---

[5]It could also be argued that while Lenz may well be satirizing the wishful endings of conventional comedy here, he might equally be 'sending up' the tragic finale of 'Romeo and Juliet', a denouement which also depends upon the deluded certainty of a disaster which has not taken place but which leads to a catastrophe as implausible as Lenz's fake happy-ending. I am grateful to my student Natalie Stapleton for this observation.

discontinuity with the main impetus of the dramatic development. He seeks also to undermine it in another equally fundamental way. As we have repeatedly emphasized, the main thrust of the dramatist's expository concern is to lay bare the dependence of the dramatic figures on the complex socio-historical forces which impinge upon their lives with an irresistible power they themselves are unable to recognize. Lenz shows that many of the tensions which the characters try to grasp in personal terms are impelled by empirical processes which affect every area of their existence. The rigour of this sceptical deterministic perception is such that it seems to exclude any possibility of inner change or of communal renewal which did not arise out of a prior far-reaching transformation of the social conditions which shape the individual's existence from the moment of his birth. The forces of Lenz's social analysis thus undermine, it seems to me, all classicist views of dramatic resolution much less the casual, derivative conciliatory gestures which form the climax of the action in *Der Hofmeister*.

The discrepancy between the suffering of the characters and their final experience of reconciliation, between the depths of their social subjection and the ease of their new beginning is blatant and irreducible, and Lenz demands that we see it as such. The sharpness of the contradiction forces us to see what in Lenz's conception is the crucial point — that the characters have not changed and are in fact incapable of change. For all they have gone through, their understanding of themselves and the world in which they live is as restricted and divided as ever. They are no nearer to grasping the nature of their involvement in the collective life of society and are thus just as deeply estranged from the roots of their behaviour.

This is perhaps most evident in the case of the Geheimer Rat. He does, it is true, show his concern to be reconciled with his son and embraces him warmly when the latter confesses his failures. 'Ich seh, ihr wilde Bursche denkt besser als eure Väter. Was hast du wohl von mir gedacht, Fritz?' (p.82). He also recognizes that Fritz and Pätus for all their unruly and unpredictable conduct have preserved their inner decency throughout. Nonetheless he is content to accept the conventional self-recriminations of his 'prodigal' son, thereby

tacitly acknowledging that the latter is to blame for the breakdown in
their relationship. Most significantly, however, the Geheimer Rat
shows no awareness of his serious failure as a father and seems to
assume during this whole encounter that his treatment of Fritz and
Gustchen has been both just and appropriate. This becomes quite
plain when his son tells him that it is his overwhelming concern for
Gustchen which has driven him to return home in this unexpected
way (p.82). Even this demonstration of the constancy of Fritz's love
does not bring the Geheimer Rat to acknowledge that he has
completely misjudged the intensity and depth of the relationship or
even to question the motives impelling his severe and unconsidered
reaction on first discovering it. Above all the Geheimer Rat still fails
to see that it was his attitude to the proclaimed love of Fritz and
Gustchen which has precipitated a series of events which were
potentially calamitous. All of this, Lenz suggests, is just part of a
greater failure. The Geheimer Rat is still unable to recognize the
force of self-deception and hypocrisy pervading his attempts to
exercise his parental responsibility. Even now after months and
months of uncertainty and some deeply distressing experiences, he is
not driven to question his aims and motives, there still seems no
crack in his self-certainty.

There is then no question of change in the Geheimer Rat. Lenz
emphasizes this while at the same time ironically affecting to ignore
it. In order to facilitate the smooth unfolding of the process of
reconciliation he deflects attention from this deeply sceptical,
deterministic presentation of the figure by superimposing upon it a
simpler, reassuring persona. In these final scenes the Geheimer Rat
appears more and more clearly in the role of a stock comic *pater
familias* who in his providential wisdom helps to bring about a
happy ending and thus to reassert the goodness of life in an ordered
beneficent world.

Lenz's portrayal of Läuffer's entry into a regenerate, fulfilling
existence is also informed by a deep, sardonic ambiguity. Here too
the dramatist shows that the change in the outer life of the character
does not arise out of a genuine inner transformation. Läuffer does
indeed appear as renewed by a vision of a life of spiritual aspiration

which surpasses sexual desire (pp.78ff.). However, Lenz emphasizes that this does not reveal a fuller understanding of his sexual nature and the processes which led to the dreadful act of self-castration. This new-found longing has in fact no root in his lived experience but appears rather as a compulsive need to undo the despair which follows from his emasculation. Lenz goes further. He shows that Läuffer's deliverance is escapist in an even more basic sense: that it is an inner, 'private' phenomenon devoid of all wider communal significance. It has no bearing at all on the anguish he has gone through in the real world of society and on the predicament of the whole group of dispossessed middle-class intellectuals to which he belongs. One of the main drives of the dramatist's expository concern throughout the play is (as we have seen) to present the figure of the tutor as the hapless victim of an oppressive and divided society. He now seems to put forward a resolution which is quite detached from, and irrevelant to, the social conditions which determined his protracted and seemingly inescapable predicament. In his liberating encounter with Lise the tutor appears suddenly as a man magically released from a destructive dilemma but (as Lenz intends us to recognize) a dilemma which recurs incessantly in contemporary society and will go on recurring unless its basic structures can be transformed.

The dramatist similarly presents the triumphant reunion of the two lovers in the final scene of the play as a grotesque parody of an accepted comic dénouement. It is true that unlike Shakespeare's star-crossed lovers, Gustchen and Fritz do find each other and renew their passionate, youthful vows with the blessings of both families (pp.65ff.). But Lenz shows that neither of the lovers has come to terms with the contradictions in which they were enmeshed or has achieved a more mature understanding of their feelings for each other. They do not overcome these contradications; it is rather as if they suddenly dissolved in the intensity of the lovers' new found happiness. Once again Lenz ironically suspends or overrules the past by suddenly and unaccountably narrowing the focus of his imaginative preoccupation. He switches attention away from the actual world of society to a sphere of conventional moralistic

concern in order, it seems, to cheer and reassure the spectator. It is
noticeable, for instance, that the Major shows no interest in the
causes of Gustchen's seduction and ensuing hopelessness or in the
nature of his own involvement as a parent in this whole horrifying
process. He seeks merely to assert the accepted proprieties. He
repeatedly declares that Gustchen deeply repents her lapse and that
she has fully expiated it in the long months of her remorseful
anguish (pp.85f.). Fritz too openly acknowledges Gustchen's failure
and emphasizes its moral seriousness, while insisting all the while
that it in no way diminishes his love for her (p.86):

> Dieser Fehltritt macht sie mir nur noch teurer — macht
> ihr Herz nur noch englischer. — Sie darf nur in den
> Spiegel sehn, um überzeugt zu sein, daß sie mein ganzes
> Glück machen werde, und doch zittert sie immer vor
> dem, wie sie sagt, ihr unerträglichen Gedanken: sie
> werde mich unglücklich machen. O was hab ich von
> einer solchen Frau anders zu gewarten als einen
> Himmel? (p.86)

The awareness of the terrible vulnerability of Gustchen which
formed a powerful focus for Lenz's socially critical enquiry, is here
denuded of all corporate significance. The dramatist now seems
intent rather on concentrating attention on Gustchen's seduction as a
single act to which she voluntarily submitted, which she now repents
and which her father and fiancé have it in their power to forgive.

This readiness to evade the burden of his pessimistic analytical
conception is also very apparent in the sly, equivocal way Lenz in
the final scene of the play takes up the long forgotten dispute about
education and places it once again in the centre of discussion. To be
sure, it seems initially as if the dramatist were just resuming a
process of critical enquiry set in motion in the opening scenes of the
play and thus achieving expository coherence. It soon becomes clear,
however, that this is just another aspect of a consistent strategy of
ironic subversion; that the dramatist is in fact again abandoning his

impelling critical preoccupations in order to evoke a specious mood of festive celebration.

In the exposition Lenz presents the question of education (as we have seen) from a diagnostic, socially critical point of view. He seeks to show that the conflict of views on schooling is a symptom of a profound division which pervades the whole life of contemporary society. Now at the very end of the dramatic action the playwright detaches the problem of education from its social context and does so in a way calculated to divert the audience from the seriousness of his earlier propagandist intention. In the general atmosphere of rejoicing the dispute about different methods of education has lost its meaning. Fritz in his happiness is able ironically to describe Gustchen's illegitimate child (which he accepts as his own) as proof of the advantages of private education (p.87). The quip is meant to express the expansive joy of the reunited lovers and their sense of a prevailing harmony which overcomes all the failure and anguish of the past. But it also serves to expose the emptiness of this experience of resolution. It blatantly glosses over the fact that none of the characters show any insight into Gustchen's predicament or the social pressures which brought it about, just as they disregard the psychological effects of her betrayal of Fritz and her pregnancy on her new life at Heidelbrunn. Here again Lenz is making it clear that he has contrived to move the action of the play out of the complex intimidating world of socio-moral conflicts into an illusory fictional realm in which mutual goodwill and the longing for happiness can suspend reality and grant the characters, whatever they have done and suffered, a completely new and blissful existence.

Throughout his presentation of the dramatic resolution Lenz emphasizes a fundamental discrepancy between his initial, socially critical concerns and the comic dénouement, between empirical perception and conventional theatrical resolution. He appears to be insisting that he has turned his back on his harsh, dissident exploration of society and yielded to the engaging and highly popular solutions of the traditional comic plot. It is as if as a writer of comedy he felt bound to offer the ending which an audience would expect and applaud, even though (or possibly precisely because) it is at odds with the impetus of the pessimistic, critical conception he set out to realize. However, he does so — he seems to be claiming — with considerable bad grace which is apparent in his offhand inconsequential plotting of events leading to the reunion of the characters and in his casual portrayal of the climactic reconciliations as banal, theatrical clichés.

The strong ironic drive to point up the discontinuity at the heart of the comic development is startlingly idiosyncratic and it is little wonder that it baffled critics in Lenz's own day and throughout the 19th century. He seems in fact to be counterposing two kinds of play, the serious, socially involved work he set out to write, and the escapist, comic fantasy he finished up by writing. The radical attempt to diagnose social antagonisms is translated as if by some unpredictable magic into a soothing quest for conciliation and ebullient joy.

4. Social Perception and Comic Form

> Keine mildernde Umstände können das
> erträglich machen, hier hilft keine
> Philosophie.[6]

Many contemporary critics were taken aback, as we have seen, by the way the action develops in *Der Hofmeister*. Some were content to express just perplexity, others, however, openly declared their complete bafflement or even outraged exasperation (*53*, pp.93ff.). For well over a century and a half little seemed to change. It is really only in the past forty years or so that scholars have come to explore Lenz's intentions in the play as a fundamental issue worthy of serious critical attention and have forced themselves to confront the crucial question: what kind of play was Lenz trying to write?

There can be no doubt, however, that *Der Hofmeister* still poses peculiar problems for critics. We only have to look at Huyssen's detailed survey of recent studies of Lenz's play to see how deeply scholars disagree with one another not just about single aspects of interpretation but more basically about the ways in which his play should be approached (*27*, pp.158ff.). And there is also an additional problem. It seems to me very noticeable that the most innovative and far-reaching general assessments of the dramatist's work in the past few decades sit uneasily on *Der Hofmeister*, his first and most idiosyncratic play. Whether scholars, like Guthke, have seen him as establishing a new integrated form of tragicomedy (*19*, pp.51ff.), or, like Hinck, as assimilating and radically reinterpreting inherited comic traditions (*23*, pp.328ff.), or, like Glaser, as realizing a satiric counterfeit of contemporary tragedy (*18*, pp.132ff.) — the

---

[6] Review of *Der Hofmeister* in *Auserlesene Bibliothek der neuesten deutschen Literatur*, 1775.

assessment in each case seems more fully appropriate to Lenz's other major comedies, *Der neue Menoza* and *Die Soldaten*, and fails to engage the distinctive formal tensions of *Der Hofmeister*. Even within the body of Lenz's work the play seems to stand as a thing apart, resisting the assumptions and judgements relevant to his other comedies.

In view of the controversies which still beset discussions of *Der Hofmeister* it seems to me best to return to very basic considerations. I would like now to try to approach the play again from the point of view of Lenz's theoretical convictions about the nature of the comic form and his understanding of his aims as a writer of comedy in the 1770s. I realize that this may involve going over some old ground but this seems to me the most effective way of coming to terms with the peculiar problems of interpretation which Lenz's play presents.

At the end of the *Annmerkungen übers Theater* Lenz seeks, somewhat hurriedly and belatedly, it seems, to outline his views of the comic mode. Comedy, he declares, is the structural inversion of tragedy. Whereas the latter is a dramatic mode informed by the driving will of the hero, comedy reflects the subjection of the dramatic figures. As a writer of comedies, he insists, his concern is overwhelmingly with the plot: 'In der Komödie gehe ich von den Handlungen aus, und lasse Personen Teil dran nehmen welche ich will' (2, p.361). Indeed, in comedy it is not necessary to know much about the characters at all, Lenz declares, because they exist merely as a function of the intrigue: 'Die Personen sind für die Handlungen da — für die artigen Erfolge, Wirkungen, Gegenwirkungen...' (2, p.361)[7].

---

[7] Lenz is here provocatively rejecting Lessing's authoritative definition of comedy in the 51st *Stück* of the *Hamburgische Dramaturgie*. Here Lessing stresses the predominance of assertive, individualized protagonists as the defining character of the genre: '...da in der Komödie die Charaktere das Hauptwerk, die Situationen nur die Mittel sind, jene sich äußern zu lassen und ins Spiel zu setzen, so muß man nicht die Situationen sondern die Charaktere in Betrachtung ziehen, wenn man bestimmen will, ob ein Stück Original oder Kopie genennt zu werden verdiene. Umgekehrt ist es in der

The foundation of the comic structure is in Lenz's view a crisis - what he terms a 'Sache' - a situation full of potentially disruptive tensions. As these unfold, so the characters are caught up willy-nilly in their momentum. The distinctive generic characteristic of the comedy is for Lenz vitality of movement, a tendency to complication and sudden reversal which lie beyond the control of the dramatic agents. The formal differences between tragedy and comedy, as Lenz presents them here, reflect opposing modes of imaginative conception, fundamentally divergent ways of apprehending existence. He assumes throughout his essay that tragedy is the only dramatic form which can embody an ultimate, metaphysical order of necessity. In enacting the free, impelling will of the sovereign individual, tragedy in his view transcends contingent, impersonal circumstance. But the tragic action, as Lenz repeatedly insists, is also exempt from arbitrary intrusive forces in another crucial respect: it is not susceptible to the pressures of the dramatist's imagination, the hidden preoccupations and pressures which shape his subjective perception of the world. The tragic development, he claims, is not at the disposal of the playwright; in a real sense it exists independently of his personal desire and purpose, beyond his reach.

This conviction underlies his paradoxical claim that French classical drama, for all its pretensions to tragic significance, is essentially comic in conception (2, pp.357ff.). As Lenz sees it, the French playwrights were striving to invoke the inexorable necessity of tragedy by taking over the fatalistic plot forms of ancient Greece. However, since they then proceeded to impose these on protagonists whom they presented as sophisticated, self-aware, moral agents, these dramatists appeared wilfully to deprive their characters of the capacity for choice and self-determination, and thus to violate the cardinal condition of tragic vision. The French classical dramatists are not tragedians, as they themselves believed, but in reality (Lenz claims) choreographers who put their unknowing, captive figures through predetermined movements, 'willkürliche Tänze' devoid of moral truth, beauty or probability.

Tragödie, wo die Charaktere weniger wesentlich sind und Schrecken und Mitleid vornehmlich aus den Situationen entspringen.' (53, pp.162f.).

Lenz's brief discussion of comedy in the *Anmerkungen übers Theater* follows directly on his sweeping condemnation of French classical tragedy. Its place in the development of Lenz's argument is surely no accident. The implied association with the mechanistic, plot-controlled pseudo-tragedy of French classicism gives a sharp satiric edge to his exposition of the determinate, circumstantial nature of the comic mode. It too is a drama of intrigue, fatalistic in its subjection of the individual agents and its undermining of the values of tragic awareness. Comedy, as much as the depersonalized heathen drama of classical France, declares the loss, the unattainability of tragedy in the modern world.

The relation of comic form to social actuality also dominates Lenz's other attempt to define the genre in his *Recension des neuen Menoza* which appeared in the *Frankfurter gelehrte Anzeiger* in 1775. Here, however, his argument takes a quite different direction. He is now concerned to bring out the immense flexibility and reach of the realistic comic mode which, unlike other dramatic kinds, seeks to embrace the life of a society (2, pp.418ff.). For this reason, Lenz argues, modern comedy is an inherently mixed, disparate form like the divided social world it reflects, and could no longer be the source of the easy, releasing enjoyment which audiences still tended to expect. The function of the form in the late 18th century was far-reaching and serious: to grasp the totality of social existence not just in its absurdity and illusion but also in its crises and antagonisms.

Lenz is acknowledging that comedy in his age, comedy as a 'mirror of society', is a deeply problematic form which has forfeited the bright, self-forgetting laughter of Plautus and the early Shakespeare. This is obviously a loss which Lenz profoundly mourned but his main aim in this essay is to stress the peculiar didactic potentiality of the new comic mode. Its range and flexibility of concern, he argues, enable the dramatist to present sombre, even distressing aspects of life to a wide audience, many of whom come to the theatre seeking only engaging comic entertainment. The writer of comedies thus had, in his view, the peculiar opportunity to extend the moral interests of spectators not yet responsive to the demands of serious drama, to educate their imaginative sensitivities in order to make them in the end capable of tragic experience.

These later reflections on comedy in the *Recension des neuen Menoza* seem both more considered and more closely related to Lenz's practical aspirations as a playwright than in his summary discussion in the *Anmerkungen*. He sees contemporary comedy here in a historical perspective which allows him to grasp its aesthetic and moral possibilities in a much more radical and constructive way. Whereas in his earlier remarks he had been content to regard comedy as a species of conventional intrigue-drama, he is intent here on emphasizing both its social immediacy and its didactic power as a primarily realistic form.

It is noticeable, however, that despite this substantial shift in critical preoccupation and tone, his discussion in the *Recension* is still shaped by the same formal assumptions which governed his earlier definition of comedy. Here, as in the *Anmerkungen*, he strives to grasp the nature of the comic mode from the point of view of its relation to tragedy which he accepts unquestioningly as the supreme dramatic form. We can also see that in both discussions Lenz regards the comic action in basically similar terms as a process which undercuts the individuality of the dramatic figures and reduces their power as moral agents. Whether he sees the protagonists in comedy as the objects of an externally controlled plot or as compelled by the impersonal forces of society, he sees them in both cases as deprived of the ability to shape their own destinies and thus as essentially untragic, or rather sub-tragic, figures.

Once we have sensed the deep shifting ambivalences which run through Lenz's theoretical statements on comedy, we are much better placed, I think, to sound the ironic discrepancies which disrupt the conception of *Der Hofmeister*, and in particular to look again at the rift between the socially determined crisis and the comic resolution which has always disconcerted commentators. We misread Lenz's intentions if we see the initial predicament of the figures (as do Guthke and his followers) as 'tragic'.[8] The thrust of all

---

[8] Guthke's definition of the essentially 'tragic' situation of Läuffer has had immense influence on discussions of *Der Hofmeister* throughout the past

Lenz's theoretical statements makes it clear that he regards the entrapment of the protagonists as serious, even calamatous, but as essentially untragic since it does not arise out of their own free actions. And because it is not tragic in this sense it lacks (again in keeping with Lenz's dramatic theories) ultimate, timeless necessity. This is the crucial point. The forces which threaten the dramatic figures are coherent and lend themselves to empirical analysis, but they are contingent and, as Lenz is out to show, can therefore be influenced or even suspended by any conjunction of circumstances which happens to impinge upon them.

The happy ending thus does not manifest the working out of any 'providential' process; it arises out of a freakish confluence of accidents and therefore, as the playwright is ironically emphasizing, could equally well not have happened. The catastrophic outcome which might have come about and the 'comic' dénouement which might not have come about, both reveal the overwhelming randomness of a world which is so unsearchable, so alien, that neither a tragic nor a comic (nor indeed any other morally significant) outcome is possible.

The 'comic' reconciliation in *Der Hofmeister* does in this way clearly expose the contingency of the crises which envelop the characters. However, the fact that these crises seem so intractable, that they reveal no inherent possibility of resolution, serves equally to point up the wishful, arbitrarily imposed nature of the conciliatory outcome. This represents a sweeping, ironic process of double

---

thirty years: 'Wenn Lenz vom *Hofmeister* als von einem "Trauerspiel" sprach, so kann er schlechterdings nichts im Sinne gehabt haben, als die dargestellte Gesamtsituation, die sich, "tragisch" auf den Hofmeister Läuffer auswirkt, der in ihr gefangen ist: rettungslos ist dieser junge Mann den demütigenden Unannehmlichkeiten seines Standes ausgesetzt; Unfreiheit, Zwang ist sein unabdingbares Los, und gleichgültig, ob wir heute dies als tragisch oder nur traurig empfinden: Lenz hat stark herausgearbeitet, daß dies im Sinne der Genie-Geistigkeit Tragische den Hofmeister mit voller Gewalt trifft ... Für die Mentalität der Stürmer und Dränger ist einem Menschen in solcher sein wesentlichstes Sein tragisch verneint.' (53, pp.139f.). This assessment seems to me to read into *Der Hofmeister* a peculiarly modern sense of the tragic which is incongruous with the shaping impulses of Lenz's creative imagination.

exposure. Lenz counterposes a sceptical analytical awareness and a vague, unfounded reconciliatory longing with a force which contrives to undermine both, and in so doing to call in question, it seems, the value of his whole dramatic enterprise.

I am very aware of the critical problem involved in interpreting *Der Hofmeister*. As far as I can see we are only able to come to terms with the formal discontinuities in the play by attributing to the author a perversely ironical, self-mocking intention which we are forced to infer from his dramaturgical theories. We are able to achieve a cohesive view of the play as a whole, only if we respect it for what it is, as the radical and deeply unsettling enactment of certain poetological conceptions which are expressed in discursive form in Lenz's idiosyncratic theory of dramatic genres.

Unless I am very much mistaken Brecht was one of the first commentators to see this problem clearly. He was very conscious of the historical importance of *Der Hofmeister* as a work of dissident, sceptically questioning realism but recognized that its ability to speak to audiences in the twentieth century was muffled by the outdated introspective literary concerns of the playwright. His attempt in 1950 to create a more accessible, socially challenging version of *Der Hofmeister* was impelled by a quest for a more simple, lucid and convincing dramatic development which could bring the polemic message of the play to full effect (5, pp.44ff.). All Brecht's main structural changes are aimed at realizing an action which is coherent, clearly and consistently motivated. He alters the development of the plot in a way which both prevents the young protagonists from coming to the very edge of disaster, and at the same time reveals clearly the causal processes leading to their deliverance. In so doing Brecht is concerned to eliminate the sharp, disruptive collision of 'tragic' and 'comic' impulses which is characteristic of Lenz's presentation of the action in favour of a more muted and above all accountable mode of presentation.

This quest for clarity of motivation is very evident, for instance, in the way Brecht portrays the rescue of Gustchen. He makes it clear that despite all her loneliness and depression she does not seriously attempt to take her own life (5, p.181). Before she sets out for the lake she leaves a clear indication of where she is going in the confident expectation that her father will be informed (5, p.180). Even as she enters the water, apparently bent on self-destruction, she is looking over her shoulder to see if help has in fact arrived.

It is also very noticeable that Brecht dispenses with Lenz's sardonic use of the lottery as the means by which Fritz and Gustchen are reunited. In his version Fritz is in Italy completing his education on the generous insistence of his father when he is overcome by a deep need to return home (5, p.198). Only when he is already well on his way to Insterburg does he receive the treacherous letter from Seiffenblase which only serves to heighten the urgency of his desire to get back as quickly as possible.

It is, however, in the presentation of Läuffer's rehabilitation that Brecht's attempt to achieve dramatic coherence and probability is most strikingly apparent. He introduces the figure of Lise into the action much earlier than in the original, and gives her a much more central role. By recasting her as Wenzeslaus' ward and housekeeper he is able to establish a close relationship between her and Läuffer from the moment the latter seeks refuge in the schoolmaster's house (5, p.174). In Brecht's version Lise is devoted to the hunted tutor from the beginning and actually risks her life in an attempt to save him when he is attacked by the Major (5, p.180). At the same time it is clear that Läuffer also feels himself drawn to the teacher's ward long before his act of self-emasculation (5, p.185).

The love which flowers between Läuffer and the naive, yearning peasant girl at the end of Brecht's version does not have the incalculable, disturbing character which it had in Lenz's original. Lise does not function here as a convenient *dea ex machina*, but appears rather as a girl who has offered Läuffer emotional support and the hope of renewal throughout, who has stood between him and the threat of lonely, engulfing despair.

All these changes which Brecht makes in the structure of the action in *Der Hofmeister* serve to make the progress of the dramatic action lucid and overseeable. They are essentially dramaturgical in character; they do not in themselves make Brecht's polemic message clearer but lend the dramatic process an inner unity and probability which are not present in the same way in Lenz's original play. While retaining by and large the dramatic framework of Lenz's play he has created a work which is quite different both in form and also in imaginative atmosphere. In his concern to create a structure of action which is free of the wantonly disruptive intrusions of Lenz's ironic conception he has brought into being a play which is certainly more open and generally accessible and shows a clear continuity of artistic purpose.

Nonetheless, it seems to me impossible to read Brecht's version of *Der Hofmeister* without a deep feeling of let-down. His controlled, intellectually distanced work has forfeited the dissonant, questing force of Lenz's original. In overcoming the breaks and discrepancies of the *Sturm und Drang* play he has also defused its abrasive exploratory power; its drive to confront different ways of seeing, to set in tension conflicting insights and expectations which is the enlivening heart of Lenz's conception.

5. Lenz and the Development of Dramatic Realism in the 19th Century

> Das Schicksal thront nicht mehr über und außer der Welt, das Schicksal ist nichts Anderes als die herrschende Weltlage selber von der jeder Einzelne abhängt; es sind die aus dieser Weltlage entspringenden Sitten, Begriffe und Zustände, die für den Einzelnen als Einzelnen durchaus undurchbrechbar und deshalb für ihn eine tragische Macht sind.
>
> Herman Hettner, *Das moderne Drama* (1851).

Der Hofmeister had next to no impact on the contemporary theatre in Germany. On the very rare occasions on which it was performed it aroused very little public or critical interest. In 1778 Friedrich Ludwig Schröder, the director of the Hamburg theatre, who had already staged productions of *Götz von Berlichingen* and Klinger's *Die Zwillinge* decided to stage a shortened and revised version of *Der Hofmeister* to mark the opening of his extensively renovated theatre. This proved to be a complete failure and the play was withdrawn after just two performances. When it was transferred to Berlin it fared even worse and had to be removed after one performance due to the unfavourable reaction of the audience (*53*, pp.110f.). In Mannheim, however, *Der Hofmeister* survived longer. It remained in the repertoire from 1780 to 1791, although it was only performed eleven times in this period.

After this the play, as far as critics have been able to establish, disappeared from the German stage for over a century. It was only in the years immediately before World War One that Arthur Kutscher, the influential director and theatre critic, succeeded in awakening a new, vital interest in the work of Lenz. Following upon his acclaimed productions of Büchner and Wedekind, he staged Lenz's plays with an energy and flair which helped establish them for the first time in the German theatre. It is probably true to say that since then they have remained a constant part, although a largely inconspicuous one, of its standard repertoire (15, pp.115ff.).

Throughout the late eighteenth and most of the nineteenth centuries Lenz fared little better at the hands of literary historians and academic critics. For the most part he was simply disregarded. When critics did examine his work closely, as for example in Hermann Hettner's *Literaturgeschichte des 18. Jahrhunderts* (1856) or Erich Schmidt's *Lenz und Klinger* (1868), this approach was deeply unsympathetic and their final assessments overwhelmingly negative (53, pp.129f.).

Yet despite all this, Lenz's work did remain known and influential throughout the nineteenth century. Although it was ignored or openly rejected by the theatrical and academic establishments it was studied and valued above all by practising playwrights, and especially by those who at different times in the course of the century felt themselves at odds with the controlling dramaturgical tradition, and sought to probe new, more rigorous forms of realism in the drama. It is noticeable that playwrights like Büchner, Hebbel, Bleibtreu and Halbe, all of whom were concerned at crucial stages of their development to bring the drama into more direct, challenging contact with direct social experience, were concerned to see their reformist endeavours in relation to what they saw as Lenz's revolutionary experiments. For all of them the plays of Lenz, and particularly *Der Hofmeister*, were a point of departure: in part a stimulus and inspiration, in part an object of critical inquiry, but most of all a fundamental, transforming essay in dramatic realism against which they could measure their own radical aspirations as playwrights.

It was Büchner who began this process of rediscovery and revaluation in the 1830s. He was not just concerned, however, to define the nature of the great historical advance which Lenz had achieved, but also to explore the imaginative possibilities it revealed and to exploit them in articulating his own compelling vision of existence in dramatic terms.

Lenz was for Büchner above all the playwright who had brought the drama into the everyday world and in so doing had swept aside at a stroke all the ossified distinctions between the beautiful and the ugly, the august and the banal. In his novella *Lenz* he presents the playwright of the *Sturm und Drang* as the supreme iconoclast of the German drama who for the first time placed the socially deprived, vulnerable individual at the very centre of imaginative concern. His Lenz is a searching realist who instinctively sees through the evasive, self-deceiving lie which is at the heart of all idealism (*4*, Vol.1). His historical achievement (as Büchner interprets it here) is that he transformed the drama into a pragmatic, questioning form, fired by the quest for close psychological observation and the recording of the day-to-day experience of recognizably ordinary people.

Büchner sees Lenz's strong incisive realism as flowing from his sympathetic involvement in the lives of the most lowly, unassuming human beings and from his power to present these as significant and moving in their own right. The eighteenth-century playwright is driven in Büchner's view by the intuitive assurance that the most basic, distinctively human emotions and desires are common to all man whatever their social or intellectual status, and that the artist is called to bring them to vibrant imaginative life. Büchner's Lenz claims that his aim in *Der Hofmeister* and *Die Soldaten* was to immerse himself in the experience of the most humble people and to recreate this in its smallest inarticulate sensations, all the time impelled by the assurance that his characters, for all their ordinariness, are fully representative human beings:

> Es sind die prosaischsten Menschen unter der Sonne; aber die Gefühlsader ist in fast allen Menschen gleich, nur ist die Hülle mehr oder weniger dicht, durch die sie brechen muß. Man muß nur Aug und Ohren dafür haben (*4*, Vol.2, pp.86f.).

Critics have consistently acknowledged the fine intuitive perceptiveness informing Büchner's appreciation of Lenz's work and no one can doubt the far-reaching influence it has enjoyed. But at the same time I think we must recognize the extent to which Büchner is seeking to clarify his own sense of artistic purpose in this confrontation with the eighteenth-century playwright and is reading, consciously or unconsciously, his own evolving preoccupations into Lenz's work. It is very obvious, for instance, that Büchner almost completely ignores the comic impetus in the conception of *Der Hofmeister* and *Die Soldaten*. He lays such emphasis on the qualities of sympathetic insight and pathos as the shaping impulses of Lenz's plays, that he remains blind to the strong satiric thrust of his creative imagination.[9] In stressing the concern of the eighteenth-century playwright to assert the essential human significance of his modest protagonists, Büchner disregards the strong ironic, belittling thrust which pervades his apprehension of the dramatic action. Lenz certainly seeks, for example, to evoke the force of anguish which drives Gustchen and Läuffer helplessly into each other's arms, but he is equally concerned (as we have seen) to show the illusory, futile character of this union in which each of the 'lovers' remains the prisoner of his own disabling fantasies (pp.31f.). In the same way Lenz seeks to reveal the despair which drives the haunted Läuffer to the horrifying act of self-mutilation (pp.60ff.). Even as he does so, however, he exposes the emptiness of this compulsive, self-punishing act which has no positive aim and robs his life of hope. Here, as so often throughout the play, Lenz is out to present developments from two colliding points of view and seeks in a

---

[9] Büchner's comments do however recall Lenz's own claims in his well-known letter to the Gräfin de la Roche shortly after his completion of *Die Soldaten* in 1776: 'Ach! das große Geheimnis, sich in viele Gesichtspunkte zu stellen, und jeden Menschen mit seinen Augen ansehen zu können! ... Sie sollten einmal ein Stück von mir lesen: Die Soldaten. Überhaupt wird meine Bemühung dahin gehen, die Stände darzustellen, wie sie sind: nicht, wie sie Personen aus einer höheren Sphäre sich vorstellen' (*35*, p.69). Here Lenz, anxious to impress the Gräfin by the force of his humane aspirations, seems to ignore the probing, ambivalent quality of his imaginative perception.

characteristically unsettling way to hold irony and pathos in sharp, unresolved tension.

We can sense here, I think, a genuine disparity. Büchner seems concerned to present Lenz as the founder of a new kind of anti-classical, democratic social tragedy. However, as we have seen, the author of *Der Hofmeister* was insistently aware that he was not a tragic playwright, that his dramatis personae were inadequate to the supreme demands of this highest literary mode and that their suffering was therefore without higher meaning and finally absurd. While Büchner senses the force of an informing tragic pathos in the helpless, uncomprehended agonies of Lenz's figures, the dramatist himself (as we have repeatedly noted) ironically evokes the echoes of tragedy only as the cruel exposing counterpoint to the intractable suffering of his characters.

Critics have paid little attention to Friedrich Hebbel's studies of Lenz's work in the late 1830s and early 1840s. They seem to me, however, both to extend the impetus of Büchner's concern and to modify it in ways which are revealing and historically important. A study of Hebbel's diaries shows that he was driven to explore Lenz's plays by the force of his deepening estrangement from the domestic drama of his time, which in its derivativeness and empty sentimentality had, in his view, become more and more artistically and socially irrelevant. He sensed in Lenz's plays a charged quality of immediacy, a driving will to confront contemporary experience in all its force and disorder. Like Büchner he sees the eighteenth-century playwright above all as a realist who was intent on developing new tragic forms which had their roots in the everyday life of society. He too seems almost completely to ignore the satiric, quizzical dimension in the conception of *Der Hofmeister* and *Die Soldaten*, and approaches them, quite intentionally, from the point of view of his own governing preoccupations as a tragic dramatist. In his discussion of both plays he consistently regards Lenz as a dramatist who was impelled by a strong intuitive sense of the rhythms of tragic development, but who repeatedly failed to achieve the stringent formal coherence of tragedy (34, pp.120ff.). The force of this unargued assumption enables him to see some aspects of

Lenz's imaginative vision with unusual sharpness, while placing some basic aspects of the dramatist's work beyond his reach.

Hebbel praises Lenz's unusual ability to bring to life convincing, psychologically discriminated characters which from the moment of their appearance on stage are vibrant with innate dramatic energy. He senses that this tense vitality of Lenz's dramatic figures stems from their rootedness in a particular social world which both confronts them and shapes their individuality (35, pp.152f.). Hebbel insists, however, that Lenz's protagonists, for all their truth to life, lack the moral substance which would enable them to fulfil the function which, as Hebbel assumes, the dramatist's tragic conception imposes on them. Characters like Gustchen or Marie Wesener in *Die Soldaten* exist, he repeatedly claims, at the mercy of their sensual impulses, and their destinies are therefore shaped not by their own responsible actions but by their accidental encounters with those who excite their desires (53, pp.125f.). Given a quite different kind of tutor, Hebbel argues sardonically, it is not impossible that Gustchen could have become not an unmarried mother but a religious recluse! There is here no necessary relation between inner selfhood and the outer development which is the heart of the tragic structure:

> Die Menschen im *Hofmeister*...finden sich zusammen wie König und Dame und Bube im Kartenspiel zusammen, und ihr Schicksal ist dann am Ende ein Kartenschicksal, eine rohe willkürliche Combination des Zufalls.. (53, p.125)

Here we can see with the ready wisdom of hindsight how close Hebbel comes to the spirit of Lenz's ironic presentation of the action in *Der Hofmeister* without sensing in the least its essentially comic potentiality. He is able to see the play only as a tragedy which has been misconceived and faultily executed.

Pervading Hebbel's discussions of Lenz's plays we can feel a constant uneasy ambivalence. Both here and in *Die Soldaten* he seems to respond imaginatively to the thrust of Lenz's analytical apprehension of events. However, when he comes to consider the plays critically, in the light of his theoretical conceptions of tragedy, he is clearly unable to accommodate this response and is driven to concentrate overwhelmingly on what he sees as inadequacies of characterization and structure. The intensity of this reaction probably reflects the urgency of his own attempts at this period to define the conception of a new kind of radical *bürgerliches Trauerspiel* which would embrace the empirical tendencies of Lenz's drama but assimilate them to higher imaginative vision: which would engage immediate actuality yet seek at the same time to aspire to genuine tragic significance (*33*, pp.100ff.).

Although he was clearly gripped by Lenz's analytical presentation of the dramatic figures, Hebbel demands that the socially entrapped hero should inwardly transcend the pressures of his situation. Despite the fact that he intuitively senses the tragic possibilities inherent in Lenz's rigorously determinist view of the action, he still asserts the moral self-responsibility of the protagonist as the essential presupposition of the tragic process.

Hebbel seems to be working his way in the early 1840s towards a form of tragedy which would fuse realistic and classicist impulses and which went far beyond the conceptions of the social drama in the *Sturm und Drang*. The innovative social tragedy which Hebbel was struggling to define would be rigorously analytical and seek to exploit new diagnostic methods of socio-psychological presentation, yet its final impetus, as he repeatedly insisted, was to surpass the circumstantial world, to subsume it in a vision of tragic necessity which was metaphysical and timeless. In Hebbel's quest for new contemporary tragic forms the plays of Lenz had a peculiar personal importance for him which he found very hard to gauge. He was keen to suggest that the first impulses towards the new social realism to which he aspired lay in the drama of the 1770s and to stress Lenz's specific achievements as a playwright. He was equally concerned, however, to expose the imaginative limitations of a work like *Der Hofmeister* and its very restricted relevance to his own original endeavours.

With the development of Naturalism in the 1880s Lenz's work achieved a new prominence. It became both more widely known and gained a more general critical standing than ever before. In Germany - in marked contrast to France - the great 'literary revolution' (as the Naturalists themselves liked to call it) took place primarily in the field of the drama, and for many of this group of young writers the plays of Lenz acquired an important symbolic as well as practical, dramaturgical significance. In their concern to stress the indigenous, 'Germanic' nature of their movement the Naturalists were very concerned to show that their quest for a radically empirical drama grew out of a long-standing, though largely inconspicuous, tradition of dramatic realism in Germany which had prevailed resiliently in the face of general critical opposition. The Naturalists consistently presented this minor tradition as a dissident, sceptical impetus which in all the different phases of its development was driven by a rejection of the central classicist tradition of German drama - a tradition which set art against life and separated the drama from the realities of social experience.

For the Naturalists, as for Büchner before them, Lenz was the first playwright in Germany, if not in Europe, to create a dramatic form dedicated to the critical observation of everyday existence. In his plays they saw the first manifestation of artistic concerns and methods which were to gain increasing prominence in the drama during the nineteenth century.

The Naturalists believed that they were the first generation of critics which was able from the vantage point of a modern positivistic view of life to grasp the full significance of Lenz's achievement as a playwright and to affirm the analytical realism he had pioneered. Critics such as Arent, Bleibtreu, Schlenther and Halbe all acknowledged Lenz's attempt to use the drama as a means of exploring the social bondage of the individual, his helpless exposure to impersonal forces, as a far-reaching anticipation of their own quest for a new 'scientific' drama. Where Hebbel, for instance, had criticized the helpless constriction of Lenz's figures as a failure of responsible tragic agency, Naturalist critics saw his perception of the drivenness of a Läuffer or Gustchen as the triumphant breakthrough of a stringent psychological realism which enabled the drama to confront life as it was. Lenz, as Bleibtreu declared in 1886, had created in *Der Hofmeister* the prototype of a new empirical kind of drama, shaped not by an adherence to the formal concepts of tragedy but by a will to penetrate the anguish of ordinary existence, to record the 'Tragik der alltäglichen Wirklichkeit' (*53*, p.132).

Some years later in 1892, when Naturalism was at its height, Halbe tried to draw together the main impulses of the Naturalists' preoccupation with Lenz's work. Halbe again emphasizes the revolutionary importance of his attempts to create tragedy out of the stuff of his own direct experience. This, Halbe insists, does not represent the drastic shortcoming earlier critics had claimed. Lenz's commitment to the everyday and the known, far from depriving his work of heightened, general significance, lent it a power of lived, authentic truth which took complete possession of the readers' emotions. When these figures speak and act, Halbe declares, we see ourselves: '...wir greifen uns an unsere Köpfe: Bist du das nicht? Sind wir das nicht, die dorten agiren?' (*53*, p.133).

There can be no doubt that the close affinity which the Naturalists felt for the work of Lenz enabled them to achieve a much fuller, more incisive understanding of his historical position as a pioneer of dramatic realism. In his plays they saw a first decisive attempt to free the genre from the maiming shackles of tradition and to probe more open, flexible forms capable of embracing the full diversity of social existence. In *Der Hofmeister* and *Die Soldaten* they recognized a new kind of 'mingled' drama which overrode false distinctions between 'high' and 'low' literary modes, and restored to the drama the power to grasp life in sharp, immediate detail. Despite all such advances in critical understanding, however, it is noticeable that the Naturalists still tended to regard Lenz primarily as a tragic dramatist and made no attempt to engage his plays as comedies. They failed consistently to respond to the ironic drive which runs through all his dramatic work, and is particularly conspicuous in *Der Hofmeister*. Nowhere do the Naturalists, for instance, seek to grasp Lenz's characteristic will to present his protagonists at once as pathetic and absurd, or to realize the dramatic action in parodistic terms as a travesty of traditional comic and tragic forms. Like their predecessors they persisted in regarding him as a dramatist with a powerful intuitive tragic sense but who lacked the artistic resilience or formal power to create the binding structures of tragedy.

Even this brief survey of critical responses to *Der Hofmeister* in the nineteenth century emphasizes again from another point of view the peculiar elusiveness of Lenz's first play. 'Progressive' commentators were certainly right to regard it as a work of a radical dramatist who, in his quest for an arresting critical realism, swept aside prevailing notions of dramatic form. Yet when interpreters like Büchner, Hebbel or Halbe, each pursuing his vision of a 'realistic' drama, attempted to get to grips with this work, they were only able to grasp some of its shaping impulses, they were unable to grasp the diversity of the converging impulses which shaped its singular conception. *Der Hofmeister*, rejected out of hand by classicist critics for over a century, proved almost as inaccessible to those who affirmed its strong experimental impetus.

Conclusion

I think we can learn a great deal from the uneasy struggles of these nineteenth-century critics to come to terms with *Der Hofmeister*. If we compare their preoccupations with those of commentators in our own day we can see at once that we, like our predecessors, are still much more at home with Lenz's play when we approach it as a work of social realism. The more closely we can relate *Der Hofmeister* to other socially critical realistic dramas in the 1770s the more assured we seem to be. It is when we are discussing the affinities between *Der Hofmeister* and plays like Wagner's *Das leidende Weib* or *Die Kindermörderin* or Schiller's *Kabale und Liebe* - all of them in their different ways innovative essays in social tragedy - that we feel most sure of our ground (*39*, pp.102ff.; *35*, pp.66ff.).

This confidence dwindles conspicuously, however, when we try to address *Der Hofmeister* as a comedy. Here we tend to become at once more tentative and more extravagant in our will to speculate. For all our greater historical awareness and more discriminated insight into the inadequacies of earlier critical approaches to the play, we are still ill at ease when we try to get to grips with the disorientating force of irony which runs through the conception of *Der Hofmeister*. Even as we acknowledge the creative power of Lenz's attempts to develop new kinds of dramatic realism, we are forced to recognize that the thrust of his comic vision is to subvert or suspend 'realistic' motivation. To do justice to *Der Hofmeister* we have to affirm the force of the dramatist's socially critical concern, while at the same time accepting a dénouement which overrules social diagnosis in an openly capricious and abrasively self-mocking way.

This fundamental discrepancy in the development of the dramatic action is, as we have already noted, at the heart of the problem of interpreting the play. I am sure, for instance, that many contemporary critics would still accept Brecht's estimate of the crucial historical importance of *Der Hofmeister* as a document of disaffected, questioning realism and would take seriously his claim that in the context of German literary developments in the 1770s it enjoys a standing comparable to that of Beaumarchais' *Le Mariage de Figaro* in French national literature (*53*, p.149). However, when Brecht puts Lenz's play forward as 'dieses deutsche Standardwerk des bürgerlichen Realismus', as a social tragedy of immense force, this would seem to evoke a work quite different in kind from *Der Hofmeister*, one which, as in Brecht's adaptation, pursues its analytical conception coherently and brings it to its shattering, relentless conclusion.

This, however, is just what Lenz ironically declines to do. He openly deflects the impetus of the dramatic development and disingenuously evades the destructive tensions laid bare in his intricate and incisive social exposition. What is more, the dramatist carries off this about-face with an insouciance which is breath-taking in its effrontery. Without warning he seems suddenly to throw over his radically deterministic conception and to remove the action from the disordered world of social existence into an escapist sphere of conventional theatrical developments which, the dramatist himself makes clear, is quite detached from everything which has gone before. Lenz seems unaccountably to give up his concern to diagnose the conditions of life in contemporary society and the whole body of assumptions which underlies his initial empirical preoccupations.

The playwright's concern to lay bare the subjection of the socially entrapped individual seems to presuppose a view of existence as a system of socio-historical processes which he can analyse and explicate. In his new search for a conciliatory resolution he abruptly abandons this analytical stance. He is now, it seems, intent on showing that the determining power of environmental forces is not a power of fate, remorseless and irresistible, but is subject, like all other phenomena, to the ultimate contingency of things. Out of the apparently inexorable momentum towards catastrophe, there emerges against all the odds a happy ending, an ending quite unpredictable since it is shaped by a freakish conjunction of circumstances beyond all possible human foresight or control.

Lenz might seem here to be claiming (teasingly, tongue-in-cheek) that the basic artistic flaws of his play - the incoherence of the dramatic development, the loss of probability and consequently of illusion - that all of these flow not from his incompetence as a playwright but from his uncompromising will to reveal the random nature of existence and are thus in a genuine sense 'realistic'. In fact, he seems to be playing off this higher, metaphysical realism against the 'rigorous' and superficially convincing, analytical mode of presentation which governed his expository concerns earlier in the play, those concerns which most impressed his contemporaries.

Comedy was the only genre available to Lenz in which he could realize his deeply personal vision of a world which seems at times to respond to man's longing for order and understanding but which in the end contrives to overwhelm both intellect and intuition by its unsearchable otherness. The sardonic thrust of his imagination is to exploit the techniques of a new analytical realism only to expose the unacknowledged ontological optimism which sustains them. His provocative concern to mimic the themes and motions of traditional tragic and comic modes appears in this context as a means of emphasizing the haphazard and opaque nature of a world finally resistant to the confident presumptions of literary form. When we look at the conception of *Der Hofmeister* from this point of view it seems to anticipate in a quite remarkable way that faceless, 'unformed' universe which Dürrenmatt describes as the home of modern comedy (34, pp.119f.): a form which embraces the tragic as a 'terrible moment' but which is unable to assimilate it to a transcendent order of significance.

Select Bibliography

A. PRIMARY TEXTS

1. J.M.R. Lenz, *Der Hofmeister oder Vorteile der Privaterziehung* (Stuttgart: Reclam, 1963).
2. ——, *Werke und Schriften*, ed. Britta Titel and Hellmuth Haug (Stuttgart: Goverts, 1966), Bd 1.
3. Johann Wolfgang Goethe, *Gesammelte Werke*, ed. E. Trunz (Hamburg: Wegner, 1949ff.).
4. Georg Büchner, *Sämtliche Werke und Briefe* (Hamburg: Wegner, 1967-71), Bd 1.
5. Bertolt Brecht, *Stücke in 12 Bänden*, ed. Elisabeth Hauptmann (Frankfurt am Main: Suhrkamp, 1959).

B. SECONDARY LITERATURE

6. C. Albert, 'Verzeihungen, Heiraten, Lotterien: der Schluß des Lenzschen *Hofmeisters*', *Wirkendes Wort*, 39 (1989), 63-71.
7. H. Arntzen, *Die ernste Komödie. Das deutsche Lustspiel von Lessing bis Kleist* (Munich: Nymphenburg, 1968).
8. P. Böckmann, *Formgeschichte der deutschen Literatur*, Bd 1 (Hamburg: Hoffmann und Campe, 1949).
9. M. Butler, 'Character and Paradox in Lenz's *Der Hofmeister*', *German Life and Letters*, 32 (1978/79), 95-103.
10. S. Damm, *Vögel, die verkünden Land. Das Leben des Jakob Michael Reinhold Lenz* (Frankfurt am Main: Insel, 1989).
11. N. Diffey, *Jakob Michael Reinhold Lenz and Jean-Jacques Rousseau* (Bonn: Bouvier, 1981).
12. E. Dosenheimer, *Das soziale Drama von Lessing bis Sternheim* (Konstanz: Südverlag, 1949).
13. B. Duncan, 'A "Cool, Medium" as social Corrective. J.M.R. Lenz's Concept of Comedy', *Colloquia Germanica*, 8 (1975), 232-45.
14. K. Eibl, '"Realismus" als Widerlegung von Literatur. Dargestellt am Beispiel von Lenz' *Hofmeister*', *Poetica*, 6 (1974), 456-67.

15. E. Genton, *Jakob Michael Reinhold Lenz et la scène allemande* (Paris: Didier, 1966).

16. R. Girard, *Lenz 1751-1792. Genèse d'une dramaturgie du tragi-comique* (Paris: Klincksieck, 1968).

17. ——, 'Lenz, ou l'inquietante étrangeté', *Etudes Germaniques*, 43 (1988), 15-24.

18. H.A. Glaser, 'Heteroklisie — der Fall Lenz', in *Gestaltungsgeschichte und Gesellschaftsgeschichte*, ed. H. Kreuzer (Stuttgart: Metzler, 1969), pp.132-51.

19. K.S. Guthke, *Geschichte und Poetik der deutschen Tragikomödie* (Göttingen: Vandenhoeck und Ruprecht, 1961).

20. J. Guthrie, *Lenz and Büchner. Studies in Dramatic Form* (Frankfurt am Main: Lang, 1984).

21. M. Halbe, 'Der Dramatiker Reinhold Lenz', *Die Gesellschaft*, 8 (1892), 568-82.

22. E. Harris, 'Structural Unity in J.M.R. Lenz's *Der Hofmeister*', *Seminar*, 8 (1972), 77-87.

23. W. Hinck, *Das deutsche Lustspiel des 17. und 18. Jahrhunderts und die deutsche Komödie* (Stuttgart: Metzler, 1965).

24. —— (ed.), *Sturm und Drang* (Kronberg: Athenäum, 1978).

25. W. Hinderer, 'Lenz. Der Hofmeister', in *Die deutsche Komödie*, ed. W. Hinck (Düsseldorf: Bloch, 1977), pp.66-88.

26. C. Hohoff, *Jakob Michael Reinhold Lenz in Selbstzeugnissen und Bilddokumenten* (Reinbek bei Hamburg: Rowohlt, 1977).

27. A. Huyssen, *Drama des Sturm und Drang. Kommentar zu einer Epoche* (Munich: Winkler, 1980).

28. E.M. Inbar, *Shakespeare in Deutschland. Der Fall Lenz* (Tübingen: Niemeyer, 1982).

29. H. Kindermann, *J.M.R. Lenz und die deutsche Romantik* (Vienna: Braumüller, 1925).

30. M.O. Kistler, *Drama of the Storm and Stress* (New York: Twayne, 1969).

31. L. Kitching,'*Der Hofmeister'. A Critical Analysis of Brecht's Adaptation of Lenz's Drama* (Munich: Winkler, 1976).

32. W. Kließ, *Sturm und Drang* (Hanover: Friedrich, 1966).

33. E. McInnes, *Das deutsche Drama des 19. Jahrhunderts* (Berlin: Erich Schmidt, 1983).

34. ——, *J.M.R. Lenz. 'Die Soldaten'. Text, Materialien, Kommentar* (Munich: Hanser, 1977).

35. ——, *'Ein ungeheures Theater'. The Drama of the Sturm und Drang* (Frankfurt am Main: Lang, 1977).

36. F. Martini, 'Die Einheit der Konzeption in J.M.R. Lenz' Anmerkungen übers Theater', *Jahrbuch der deutschen Schillergesellschaft*, 14 (1970), 159-82.

37. G. Mattenklott, *Melancholie in der Dramatik des Sturm und Drang* (Stuttgart: Metzler, 1968).
38. H. Mayer, *Bertolt Brecht und die Tradition* (Pfullingen: Neske, 1961).
39. J. Osborne, *J.M.R. Lenz. The Renunciation of Heroism* (Göttingen: Vandenhoeck und Ruprecht, 1975).
40. F.B. Parkes, *Epische Elemente in J.M.R. Lenzs Drama 'Der Hofmeister'* (Göppingen: Heinz, 1973).
41. R. Pascal, *The German Sturm und Drang* (Manchester: Manchester University Press, 1953).
42. W.H. Preuß, *Selbstkastration oder Zeugung neuer Kreatur. Zum Problem der moralischen Freiheit in Leben und Werk von J.M.R. Lenz* (Bonn: Bouvier, 1983).
43. M.N. Rosanow, *Jakob M.R. Lenz, der Dichter der Sturm und Drang Periode* (Leipzig: Schulze, 1909).
44. O. Rudolf, *Jakob Michael Reinhold Lenz. Moralist und Aufklärer* (Bad Homburg: Gehlen, 1970).
45. K. Scherpe, 'Dichterische Erkenntnis und "Projektmacher"', *Goethe-Jahrbuch*, 94 (1977), 206-35.
46. A. Schöne, *Säkularisation als sprachbildende Kraft. Studien zur Dichtung deutscher Pfarrersöhne* (Göttingen: Vandenhoeck und Ruprecht, 1958).
47. B.A. Sørensen, *Herrschaft und Zärtlichkeit. Der Patriarchalismus und das Drama im 18. Jahrhundert* (Munich: Beck, 1984).
48. M. Spalter, *Brecht's Tradition* (Baltimore: Johns Hopkins University Press, 1967).
49. W. Stammler, *'Der Hofmeister' von J.M.R. Lenz. Ein Beitrag zur Literatur des 18. Jahrhunderts* (Diss. Halle, 1908).
50. I. Stephan und H.-G. Winter, *'Ein verübergehendes Meteor?' J.M.R. Lenz und seine Rezeption in Deutschland* (Stuttgart: Metzler, 1984).
51. H. Stipa-Madland, *Non-Aristotelian Drama in Eighteenth Century Germany and its Modernity: J.M.R. Lenz* (Frankfurt am Main: Lang, 1982).
52. C. Stockmeyer, *Soziale Probleme im Drama des Sturm und Drangs* (Frankfurt am Main: Gerstenberg, 1922).
53. Voit, Friedrich (ed.), *J.M.R. Lenz, 'Der Hofmeister'. Erläuterungen und Dokumente* (Stuttgart: Reclam, 1986).
54. H.-G. Winter, *J.M.R. Lenz* (Stuttgart: Metzler, 1987).